Functional Skills

Maths

Level 2

This book is for anyone doing Level 2 Functional Skills Maths.
It covers everything you need, whichever exam board you're studying.

All the topics are explained in a straightforward way, with test-style
questions to give you plenty of realistic practice before the final test.

Since 1995, CGP study books have helped millions of students do well
in their tests and exams. We cover dozens of subjects for all ages
— and we always keep our prices as low as possible.

Study & Test Practice

Contents

Section One — Number

Adding and Subtracting 1

Multiplying and Dividing 3

Using a Calculator 6

The Number Line and Scales 8

Fractions 11

Mixed Fractions 14

Decimals 16

Percentages 20

Fractions, Decimals and Percentages 23

Proportion 26

Ratios 27

Scaling Up and Down 30

Formulas in Words 32

More Formulas 34

Section Two — Measure

Units 39

Length and Perimeter 43

Working with Lengths 46

Areas of Squares and Rectangles 49

Areas of Triangles and Circles 51

More on Area 53

Volume 56

Money 58

Time 63

Timetables 67

Section Three — Shape and Space

2D and 3D Objects 70

Symmetry 75

Plans 77

Maps and Map Scales 80

Section Four — Handling Data

Tables 82

Drawing Tables 86

Bar Charts 89

Line Graphs 92

Other Charts and Graphs 95

Drawing Charts and Graphs 97

Interpreting Data 101

Averages 104

Range 107

Using Averages and Range 108

Probability 110

Test-style Questions

Test Help 113

Task 1 — Banking and Finance 114

Task 2 — Landscape Gardening 119

Task 3 — Health and Fitness 123

Task 4 — Going Out 125

Task 5 — Decorating 130

Task 6 — A Car Boot Sale 133

Task 7 — City Planning 136

Task 8 — A Christmas Fair 141

Answers 144

Glossary 152

Index 155

Published by CGP

Editors:
Katie Braid, Jane Ellingham, Christopher Lindle, Hayley Thompson.

Contributor:
George MacDonald.

With thanks to Anna Gainey, Rosie McCurrie and David Norden for the proofreading.

ISBN: 978 1 84762 872 5

Groovy website: www.cgpbooks.co.uk

Printed by Elanders Ltd, Newcastle upon Tyne.
Jolly bits of clipart from CorelDRAW®

Adding and Subtracting

You Need to Know When to Add or Subtract

1) The questions you get in your assessment will be based on real-life situations.

2) You won't always be told whether to add or subtract (take away).

3) You'll need to work out for yourself what calculation to do.

Example 1

Joe is booking a holiday. Everything he has to pay for is shown below.
He gets £50 off the total cost of his holiday for booking online.

How much will the holiday cost Joe?

Flights	£299
7 nights in a 4* hotel	£345
Airport transfers	£40

Step 1 — add up the prices of the flights, hotel and airport transfers:

299 + 345 + 40 = £684 ← Use a calculator to work this out. You'll be able to take a calculator into the test and use it whenever you need to.

Step 2 — take away £50 from your answer:

684 − 50 = £634

Sometimes you need to include units in your answer. Units tell you what type of number you've got. In this case the units are '£'.

Example 2

Kerry has £400. She needs to pay £110 in council tax and £246 for her electricity bill. She also wants to buy a new coat for £50.

Will Kerry have enough money left for the coat once she has paid her bills? Explain your answer.

You need to take away £110 and £246 from £400, then see how much is left.

400 − 110 − 246 = £44

Kerry only has £44 left once she has paid her bills so, no, she doesn't have enough money left for the coat.

2

Always Check Your Answer

1) Adding and subtracting are opposite calculations.

2) Once you've got your answer, you can check it using the opposite calculation.

3) You should get back to the number you started with.

Example 1

What is 456 – 334?   Answer: 456 – 334 = 122

Check it using the opposite calculation: 122 + 334 = 456

Example 2

What is 92 + 25?

Answer: 92 + 25 = 117

You only need to do one of these calculations to check your answer.

Check it using the opposite calculation: 117 – 25 = 92   OR   117 – 92 = 25

Practice Questions

1) 7643 people went to a football match in Manchester. 6391 people went to a football match in Glasgow. How many people went to these two football matches in total?

....

2) 250 people work for PFC textiles. 96 are women. How many are men?
Show how you can check your answer.

....

....

3) Zainab buys a dress for £36 and a new pair of shoes for £28. She has a voucher for £5 off her final bill. How much does Zainab spend using the voucher?

....

....

4) Doug gets 25 days of holiday each year. He used 6 days of holiday at Christmas and 4 days at Easter. He wants to take 10 days for his summer holiday.
Does he have enough holiday left? Explain your answer.

....

....

Section One — Number

Multiplying and Dividing

You Need to Know When to Multiply or Divide

You'll get questions where you need to multiply or divide.
You need to be able to work out what calculation to do for yourself.

Example 1

Jan needs to buy 100 large envelopes at 76p each.
How much money does she need?

Answer: each envelope costs 76p. So you need to work out 100 times 76.

$$100 \times 76 = 7600p \text{ or } £76.00$$

Example 2

A pub quiz team has five players. The team wins £40 prize money, to be split equally between the players. How much will each player be given?

Answer: the £40 has to be divided between 5 players.
So you need to divide 40 by 5.

$$40 \div 5 = £8$$

Always Check Your Answer

1) Multiplying and dividing are opposite calculations.

2) Once you've got your answer, you can check it using the opposite calculation.

3) You should get back to the number you started with.

Example

What is 32×9?

Answer: $32 \times 9 = 288$

Check it using the opposite calculation: $288 \div 9 = 32$ OR $288 \div 32 = 9$

4

1) Kathy has 750 g of cake mixture. She wants to divide it evenly between 3 tins.
   How much cake mixture should go into each tin?

   ....

2) A newsagent buys 100 chocolate bars for £32. How much should he sell each chocolate bar
   for to make his money back? Show how you can check your answer.

   ....

   ....

3) Jake buys 12 bunches of roses for £2 a bunch. He sells all 12 bunches at £7 a bunch.

   a)   How much did Jake spend on the roses in total?

   ....

   b)   How much did Jake sell the roses for in total?

   ....

You Need to Know How to Square a Number

1) To square a number, you just multiply the number by itself.

   Examples

   7 squared = 7 × 7 = 49.   15 squared = 15 × 15 = 225.

2) You can write squared numbers like this: $\longrightarrow x^2$
   Where x is a number and ^{2} means 'squared'.

   Examples

   7 squared can be written as 7^2.   15 squared can be written as 15^2.

3) If your calculator has a button with x^2 on it, you can use it to square a number.

   Example

   What is 8^2?

   Press: | 8 | | x^2 | | = | 64 ⟵ *If your calculator doesn't have the x^2 button, just do 8 × 8.*

Some Questions Need Answers that are Whole Numbers

1) Real-life division questions can be tricky.
   You won't always end up with a whole number.

2) But sometimes, you'll need to give a whole number as your answer.

Example 1

Glenn is laying a patio in his back garden. He needs 27 slabs
for the patio and they are available in packs of 5 slabs.
How many packs does Glenn need to buy?

Calculation: $27 \div 5 = 5.4$

He can't buy 5.4 packs, so you need to give your answer
as a whole number.

5.4 is between 5 and 6. There aren't enough slabs in 5 packs.
So Glenn will have to buy **6 packs** and have 3 slabs extra.

Example 2

Tina uses 2 m² of material to make a dress. How many dresses can
she make out of 11 m² of material?

Calculation: $11 \div 2 = 5.5$

You can't have 5.5 dresses, so you need to give your answer as a
whole number.

5.5 is between 5 and 6. There isn't enough material for 6 dresses.
So Tina will only be able to make **5 dresses**.

Practice Questions

1) What is:

   a) 17 squared?

   b) 44^2?

2) A large egg box holds 12 eggs. Flynn has 26 eggs.
   How many large egg boxes does he need to carry them?

3) A group of 14 friends are going on holiday. They can fit 4 people in a car.
   How many cars do they need to take all 14 people?

Using a Calculator

Calculations with Several Steps

1) You'll sometimes need to do calculations that have several steps.

2) You could work out each step separately or you could type the whole thing into your calculator in one go.

3) BUT you need to be careful about how you type things into your calculator.

Some Calculators Use Brackets (...)

1) Some calculators use brackets to help them work out calculations with several steps.

2) The brackets tell the calculator to work out the bits inside the brackets before it does the rest of the calculation.

3) Without them, the calculator does the calculation in the wrong order — and you get the wrong answer.

Example

Claire works for 4 hours a week in a shop. She works for 6 hours a week in a nursery. How many hours does Claire work in total in 4 weeks?

1) You could work out the total number of hours Claire works in a week, then times this by 4.

Total number of hours Claire works in a week = 4 + 6 = 10

Total number of hours Claire works in 4 weeks = 10 × 4 = **40 hours**

2) You could also do the whole calculation in one go on your calculator.

But if you type in '4 + 6 × 10', you might get the wrong answer.

If so, your calculator probably uses brackets.

You need to tell the calculator to work out the total number of hours a week Claire works first, then times this by 4.

So you need to put 4 + 6 in brackets:

$$(4 + 6) \times 4 = 40 \text{ hours}$$

Brackets always come in pairs.

Calculators Without Brackets

Not all calculators use brackets. You still need to be careful about how you type calculations into your calculator though.

Example

What is 22 divided by the total of 5 + 6?

1) Work out what 5 + 6 is first, then divide 22 by this number: 5 + 6 = 11

$$22 \div 11 = \mathbf{2}$$

2) If you just type '22 ÷ 5 + 6' into your calculator, you'll get the wrong answer:

$$22 \div 5 + 6 = 10.4$$

So, if your calculator doesn't have bracket buttons, it's best to work out each step of the calculation separately.

If your calculator doesn't have bracket buttons and you're given a calculation that has brackets in, just work out the bits in brackets first.

Example

What is 36 ÷ (3 × 4)?

1) Work out the bit in brackets first: 3 × 4 = 12

2) Put this answer into the calculation instead of the brackets: 36 ÷ 12 = **3**

Practice Questions

1) What is 12 ÷ (2 × 3)?

....

2) What is (11 × 24) ÷ (4 × 3)?

....

3) What is (102 ÷ 3) ÷ (50 ÷ 25)?

....

4) Omar drives 10 miles to work every day. He drives 11 miles home to avoid traffic. He does this 5 days a week. How far does Omar drive in a week?

....

....

The Number Line and Scales

Negative Numbers are Less than Zero

1) A negative number is a number less than zero.

2) You write a negative number using a minus sign (-). For example, -1, -2, -3.

3) A number line is really useful for understanding negative numbers.

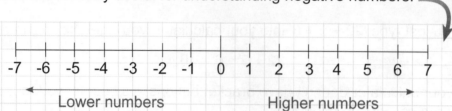

All negative numbers are to the left of zero.

All positive numbers are to the right of zero.

The further right you go, the higher the numbers get.
For example, -2 is higher than -7.

Use a Number Line to Work Out Differences

You can use a number line to work out the difference between two numbers.
For example, the difference between a positive number and a negative number.

Example

A fridge is 2 °C. A freezer is -7 °C.   What is the difference in temperature between the fridge and the freezer?

1) Draw a number line that includes both the numbers in the question.

2) Count back from 2 to -7 °C.

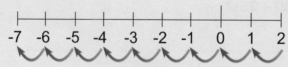

There are 9 steps, so the difference in temperature is 9 °C.

Practice Questions

1) A test has negative marking. Ian scores -2. Jess scores -14. Who has the lowest score?

   ....

   ....

2) Rachael has -£346 in her bank account. Larry has -£334 in his bank account.

   a) Who has less money in their account?

   ....

   ....

   b) Rachael is given £15. How much money does she now have in her account?

   ....

3) The temperature in Moscow -8 °C. In Berlin it is 4 °C.
   What is the difference between these two temperatures?

   ....

   ....

A Scale is a Type of Number Line

1) You might be asked to read a scale.
   For example, to read the temperature off a thermometer.

2) Scales are just number lines.
   They don't always show every number though.

Example 1

This is part of a thermometer.
It shows the temperature in °C.

What temperature is it?

Answer:

There are 4 lines between 0 and -5.
So each line must be worth 1 °C.

It is -3 °C.

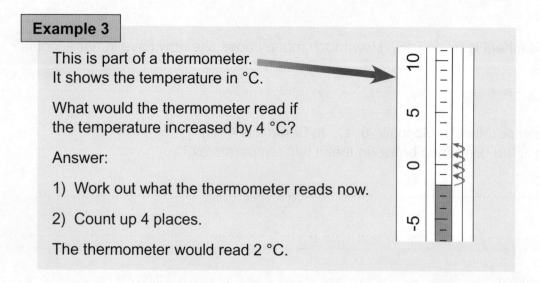

Example 2

This is part of a thermometer.
It shows the temperature in °C.

What would the thermometer read if
the temperature dropped by 5 °C?

Answer:

1) Work out what the thermometer reads now.

2) Count down 5 places.

The thermometer would read -6 °C.

Example 3

This is part of a thermometer.
It shows the temperature in °C.

What would the thermometer read if
the temperature increased by 4 °C?

Answer:

1) Work out what the thermometer reads now.

2) Count up 4 places.

The thermometer would read 2 °C.

Practice Questions

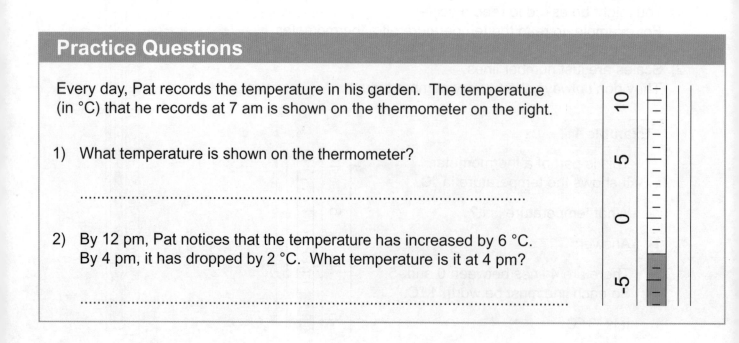

Every day, Pat records the temperature in his garden. The temperature
(in °C) that he records at 7 am is shown on the thermometer on the right.

1) What temperature is shown on the thermometer?

....

2) By 12 pm, Pat notices that the temperature has increased by 6 °C.
By 4 pm, it has dropped by 2 °C. What temperature is it at 4 pm?

....

Fractions

Fractions Show Parts of Things

1) If something is divided up into equal parts, you can show it as a fraction.

2) There are two bits to every fraction:

The bottom number shows how many parts there are in total. → $\dfrac{2}{5}$ ← The top number shows how many parts you're talking about.

Example

A pizza is cut into 9 slices. 2 slices are eaten.
What fraction of slices were eaten?

2 out of the 9 slices were eaten, so it's $\dfrac{2}{9}$ (you say 'two ninths').

Learn How to Write Fractions

Here's how to write some common fractions:

One half = $\dfrac{1}{2}$ One third = $\dfrac{1}{3}$

One quarter = $\dfrac{1}{4}$ Three quarters = $\dfrac{3}{4}$

Practice Question

1) 13 people take their driving test on the same day. 9 pass.

   a) What fraction of people passed?

   ....

   b) What fraction of people failed?

   ....

'Of' means 'times'

1) Sometimes, you might need to calculate a 'fraction of' something.

2) In these cases, 'of' means 'times' (multiply).

Example 1

What is $\frac{1}{8}$ of 64?

1) 'Of' means 'times' (×), so $\frac{1}{8}$ of 64 is the same as $\frac{1}{8} \times 64$.

2) You type fractions into your calculator by dividing the top by the bottom.

So $\frac{1}{8} = 1 \div 8$

3) The overall calculation you need to do is: $1 \div 8 \times 64 = 8$

Example 2

A survey asks 96 people whether they are satisfied with their job. A third of the people asked say 'no'. How many people say no?

You need to calculate one third of 96.

1) 'Of' means 'times' (×), so $\frac{1}{3}$ of 96 is the same as $\frac{1}{3} \times 96$.

2) $1 \div 3 \times 96 = 32$ So 32 people said no.

Practice Questions

1) What is $\frac{1}{4}$ of 48? ....

2) What is $\frac{2}{11}$ of 55? ....

3) A hair salon has 24 clients booked in for the week.

   a) One sixth of the clients cancel their appointments. How many clients cancel?

   ....

   b) Of the remaining clients, two fifths are booked in for a cut and colour. How many clients are booked in for a cut and colour?

   ....

   ....

Discounts Involving Fractions

You might need to calculate a fraction of a price to work out a discount price.

Example 1

A coat usually costs £75. In the sale, it's half price.
What is the sale price of the coat?

This is just like saying that the coat costs 'half of £75' in the sale.

So you need to work out: $\frac{1}{2} \times 75$

$1 \div 2 \times 75 = £37.50$ So the sale price of the coat is **£37.50**.

Sometimes you need to add or subtract a fraction of a price to work out the discount price.

Example 2

A cruise usually costs £1200. A special offer gives two thirds off the price.
What is the special offer price of the cruise?

1) First you need to work out two thirds of £1200.
This is the same as $\frac{2}{3} \times 1200$.

$2 \div 3 \times 1200 = £800$ So the special offer gives £800 off the cruise.

2) Then you need to take this number away from £1200: $1200 - 800 = £400$
So the special offer price is **£400**.

Practice Questions

1) A pair of boots normally cost £40 but are half price in the sale. How much do they now cost?

$\frac{1}{2} \times 40 = 1 \div 2 \times 40 = 20$

2) A fast food chain has reduced the size of their burgers. Each burger used to weigh 540 g.
They're now a third smaller. What does each burger weigh now?

$\frac{1}{3} \times 540 = 1 \div 3 \times 54 = £180$

$540 - 180 = 360 \text{ g}$

3) A fitted kitchen costs £2000. The price is reduced by a quarter in the sale.
The new price is then reduced by a third. How much does the kitchen now cost?

$\frac{1}{4} \times 2000 = 1 \div 4 \times 2000 = 500$ $500 - 2000 = 1500$

$\frac{1}{3} \times 1500 = 1 \div 3 \times 1500 = 500$

$1500 - 500 = 1000$

Mixed Fractions

Mixed Fractions

1) Mixed fractions are when you have whole numbers and fractions together. For example, $1\frac{1}{4}$ (one and a quarter).

2) You can enter a mixed fraction into your calculator by typing in the fraction first, and then adding the whole number.

> **Example**
>
> To enter $1\frac{1}{4}$, type in: $1 \div 4 + 1 = 1.25$ ← *This gives you the fraction as a decimal. See page 16 for more on decimals.*

Calculations Involving Mixed Fractions

You might get asked to do a calculation involving a mixed fraction.

> **Example 1**
>
> What is $5\frac{1}{2} \times 4$?
>
> 1) Start by entering $5\frac{1}{2}$ into your calculator: ⟶ $1 \div 2 + 5 = 5.5$
>
> 2) Then multiply your answer by 4: ⟶ $5.5 \times 4 = \mathbf{22}$

> **Example 2**
>
> Dee is picking apples. She picks 9 kg of apples and puts them into crates. Each crate weighs $1\frac{1}{2}$ kg when full. How many crates does Dee use?
>
> Answer:
>
> You need to divide the total weight of apples by the weight of a crate: $9 \div 1\frac{1}{2}$.
>
> 1) Enter $1\frac{1}{2}$ into your calculator: ⟶ $1 \div 2 + 1 = 1.5$
>
> 2) Then divide 9 by this number: ⟶ $9 \div 1.5 = 6$
>
> So Dee needs to use **6 crates**.
>
> If your calculator has brackets, you can do this calculation in one go. Just press: $9 \div (1 \div 2 + 1) = 6$

Example 3

Fiona is driving from Penrith to Manchester.
She needs to stop at Kendal on the way to pick up her friend Steve.

The journey from Penrith to Kendal will take half an hour.
The journey from Kendal to Manchester will take $1\frac{1}{2}$ hours.

How long will the journey take in total?

Answer: you need to add together $\frac{1}{2}$ hour and $1\frac{1}{2}$ hours.

1) Enter the $1\frac{1}{2}$ into your calculator: ⟶ $1 \div 2 + 1 = 1.5$

2) Then add the $\frac{1}{2}$: ⟶ $1 \div 2 + 1.5 = 2$ hours

If your calculator has brackets, you can do this calculation in one go.
Just press: $(1 \div 2) + (1 \div 2 + 1) = 2$ hours

Practice Questions

1) What is $6\frac{1}{4} \times 3$? $(1 \div 4 + 6) \times 3 = 18.75$

2) What is $9\frac{1}{2} \div 2$? $(\frac{1}{2} + 9) \div 2 = 4.75$

3) Harry wants to take the train from Barrow to Carlisle. A direct train will take $2\frac{1}{2}$ (2.5) hours.

   If Harry changes at Lancaster, it will take 1 hour to get from Barrow to Lancaster and
   $\frac{3}{4}$ of an hour to get from Lancaster to Carlisle.

   He'll also have to wait for $\frac{1}{2}$ an hour in Lancaster station.

   Is it quicker for Harry to get the direct train or change at Lancaster? Explain your answer.

   $1\frac{3}{4} + \frac{1}{2} = 2\frac{1}{4}$

Decimals

Not All Numbers Are Whole Numbers

1) Decimals are numbers with a decimal point (.) in them. For example, 0.5, 1.3.

2) They're used to show the numbers in between whole numbers.

Examples

The number 32.1 is a bit bigger than the number 32.

The number 32.9 is a bit smaller than the number 33.

The number 32.5 is exactly halfway between the numbers 32 and 33.

3) You can show decimals on a number line.

Example

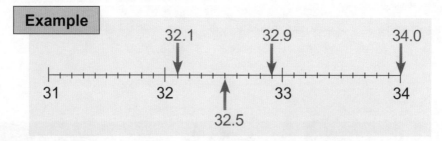

Rounding off Decimals

1) You can sometimes get an answer with lots of numbers after the decimal point.

2) Instead of writing down the whole thing, you can shorten the answer and only write down one or two numbers after the decimal point. This is called rounding off.

3) To round off you need to decide how many numbers you want after the decimal point.

4) Then you need to look at the next number along (the decider). If this is less than five you can just leave it off (and all the numbers after it) when you write down your answer.

Examples

1) Round 2.8427865 so that there are two numbers after the decimal point (this is called rounding to two decimal places).

You want two numbers after the decimal point, so the decider is the third number after the decimal point. The decider is 2, which is less than 5. So the answer is **2.84**

2) Round 10.341346786 to one decimal place.

You want one number after the decimal point, so the decider is the second number after the decimal point. The decider is 4, which is less than 5. So the answer is **10.3**

You May Need to Change the Last Number When Rounding

If the decider is 5 or more, then you need to add 1 to the last number when you round off.

Examples

1) Round 9.3186895 to two decimal places.

   You want two numbers after the decimal point, so the decider is the third number after the decimal point. The decider is 8, which is more than 5, so you need to add 1 to the last number.

   So the answer is **9.32**

2) Round 20.85373122 to one decimal place.

   You want one number after the decimal point, so the decider is the second number after the decimal point. The decider is 5, so you need to add 1 to the last number.

   So the answer is **20.9**

How to Put Decimals in Order

You might need to arrange a list of decimal numbers in order of size.

Example

Put these decimals in order of size: 1.22, 0.24, 0.06, 0.3.
Start with the smallest.

1) Put the numbers into a column, lining up the decimal points.

2) Make all the numbers the same length by filling in extra zeros at the ends.

3) Look at the numbers before the decimal point.
   Arrange the numbers from smallest to largest.

4) If any of the numbers are the same, move onto the numbers after the decimal point. Arrange the numbers from smallest to largest.

Step 1:	Step 2:	Step 3:	Step 4:
1.22	1.22	0.24	0.06
0.24	0.24	0.06	0.24
0.06	0.06	0.30	0.30
0.3	0.30	1.22	1.22

The order is: 0.06, 0.24, 0.3, 1.22.

Adding and Subtracting Decimals

1) You can add and subtract decimals using a calculator.

2) It's exactly the same as with whole numbers — just remember to type the decimal point into the calculator.

Example 1

Julie is a solicitor. She charges her clients by the hour. She works on a case for 2.5 hours on Monday, 1.25 hours on Tuesday and 0.75 hours on Wednesday. How many hours should she charge her clients for in total?

Answer: add together all the hours Julie has worked on the case.

2.5 + 1.25 + 0.75 = **4.5 hours**

Example 2

Clyde wants to know how much his sunflower has grown. It used to measure 1.45 m. It now measures 1.72 m. How much has it grown?

Answer: take away the first height (1.45 m) from the second height (1.72 m).

1.72 − 1.45 = **0.27 m**

Multiplying and Dividing Decimals

You can multiply and divide decimals in exactly the same way as whole numbers.

Example 1

Alwen is holding a charity event. She made £665.50 from ticket sales and sold 121 tickets. How much did each ticket cost?

Answer: divide the money made from the ticket sales by the number of tickets sold.

665.50 ÷ 121 = **£5.50**

Example 2

James earns £6.40 an hour and works 28.5 hours a week. How much money does he earn in a week?

Answer: multiply the amount James earns in an hour by the number of hours he works in a week.

6.40 × 28.5 = **£182.40**

Practice Questions

1) Round 3.57896 so that there is one number after the decimal point.

   ...3.6...

2) Round 1.024 so that there are two numbers after the decimal point.

   ...1.2...

3) Put these distances in order of size: 1.2 km, 1.75 km, 1.05 km, 1.25 km.
   Start with the smallest.

   ....

4) A gymnast needs 44 points or more to win a competition. She scores 14.7 in her first event,
   15.2 in her second event and 13.9 in her third event. Does she have enough points to win?
   Explain your answer.

   ....

   ....

5) Tom has £262.98 in his bank account. He pays in a cheque for £56.23, then spends £39.47
   on petrol and £41.42 in the supermarket. How much money is left in his account?

   ....

   ....

6) Jeremy works 37.5 hours a week. He needs to divide this time equally between
   two different projects. How many hours should he spend on each project?

   ....

7) A company has 178 staff members. It costs the company a total of £142.40 to provide lunch
   for its staff. How much does the company spend on lunch per staff member?

   ....

8) Rose buys 3 magazines for £1.75 each. She also buys 2 drinks for £1.32 each.
   How much does she spend in total?

   ..$(3 \times 1.75) + (2 \times 1.32) = 7.89$..

   ....

Percentages

Understanding Percentages

1) 'Per cent' means 'out of 100'.

2) % is a short way of writing 'per cent'.

3) So 20% means twenty per cent. This is the same as 20 out of 100.

4) You can write any percentage as a fraction.   There's more on fractions on page 11.

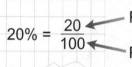

$20\% = \dfrac{20}{100}$ ← Put the percentage on the top of the fraction.

← Put 100 on the bottom of the fraction.

Calculating Percentages

1) Sometimes, you might need to calculate the 'percentage of' something.

2) In these cases, 'of' means 'times' (multiply).

Example 1

What is 30% of 96?

1) Write it down: 30% of 96
                           ↓   ↓ ↓

2) Turn it into maths: $\dfrac{30}{100}$ × 96

3) Work it out: 30 ÷ 100 × 96 = 28.8

Example 2

A restaurant has 60 tables. 25% of the tables have been reserved.
How many tables have been reserved?

1) Write it down: 25% of 60
                           ↓   ↓ ↓

2) Turn it into maths: $\dfrac{25}{100}$ × 60

3) Work it out: 25 ÷ 100 × 60 = 15 tables

Practice Questions

1) What is 16% of 48?

$16 \div 100 \times 48 =$

2) What is 40% of 660?

$40 \div 100 \times 660 =$

3) A flight from London to Madrid has 300 passengers. 3% of the passengers are vegetarian. How many passengers are vegetarian?

$3 \div 100 \times 300 =$

4) Asif is a dentist. He sees 75 patients in a week. Of these, 28% need to have a filling. How many patients need a filling?

$28 \div 100 \times 75 =$

5) Lauren is buying a house for £98 000. She needs a deposit of 15%. How much money does Lauren need for the deposit?

$15 \div 100 \times 98000 =$

Calculating Percentage Increase

1) Sometimes, you might need to calculate a percentage increase.

2) If so, you need to find the 'percentage of' first.
   Then you add it on to the original number.

Example

In 2009 a town's population was 2500. By 2012, it had increased by 6%. How many people live in the town in 2012?

Answer:

1) Find 6% of 2500: $\frac{6}{100} \times 2500 = 6 \div 100 \times 2500 = 150$

2) Add this on to 2500: $2500 + 150 = 2650$

So, 2650 people live in the town in 2012.

Calculating Percentage Decrease

1) You might also need to calculate a percentage decrease.

2) First you find the 'percentage of'. Then you take it away from the original number.

Example

Last year a company made a profit of £20 000. This year, profits are down by 12%. How much profit did the company make this year?

Answer:

1) Find 12% of £20 000: $\frac{12}{100} \times 20\,000 = 12 \div 100 \times 20\,000 = £2400$

So the company made £2400 less profit.

2) Take this away from £20 000: $20\,000 - 2400 = £17\,600$

The company made **£17 600** profit.

Practice Questions

1) Penny is the manager of a retail outlet. The outlet offers a 40% discount on designer clothes. If a dress normally costs £120, how much should Penny sell it for?

$40 \div 100 \times 120 = 48$

$120 - 48 = 72$

2) Jim earns £21 000 a year. He's given a pay rise of 2%. How much will Jim earn after his pay rise?

$2 \div 100 \times 21\,000 = 420 + 21\,000 = 21\,420$

3) A company made a profit of £35 000 last year. This year, its profits have increased by 5%. How much profit did the company make this year?

$5 \div 100 \times 35 = 1750 + 35\,000 = 36\,750$

4) In January, a florist took orders from 260 customers. In February, orders were up by 75%. How many customers placed an order in February?

$75 \div 100 \times 260 = 195 + 260 = 455$

Fractions, Decimals and Percentages

These Fractions, Decimals and Percentages Are All the Same

The following fractions, decimals and percentages all mean the same thing.

They're really common, so it's a good idea to learn them.

$\frac{1}{2}$ is the same as 0.5, which is the same as 50%.

$\frac{1}{4}$ is the same as 0.25, which is the same as 25%.

$\frac{3}{4}$ is the same as 0.75, which is the same as 75%.

$\frac{1}{1}$ is the same as 1, which is the same as 100%.

You Can Change Fractions into Percentages

To change a fraction into a percentage you should:

1) Multiply the fraction by 100.   2) Add a per cent (%) sign.

Example 1

What is $\frac{2}{5}$ as a percentage?

1) Multiply the fraction by 100: $2 \div 5 \times 100 = 40$

2) Add a % sign = 40%

Example 2

9 out of 10 people surveyed are against the closure of a local swimming pool. What percentage is this?

1) 9 out of 10 as a fraction is $\frac{9}{10}$

2) Multiply the fraction by 100: $9 \div 10 \times 100 = 90$

3) Add a % sign = 90%

You Can Also Convert Fractions into Decimals

1) To convert a fraction into a decimal you should:

Divide the top number in the fraction by the bottom number.

Example

What is $\frac{2}{5}$ as a decimal?

Answer: divide 2 by 5. $2 \div 5 = 0.4$

2) In your assessment, you might be asked to give a fraction in its 'simplest form'. This just means writing a fraction involving big numbers in the simplest way possible.

3) One way to do this is by converting the fraction into a decimal.

Example

Give the fraction $\frac{2500}{5000}$ in its simplest form.

Answer: convert the fraction into a decimal by dividing 2500 by 5000.

$2500 \div 5000 = 0.5$

Practice Questions

1) a) What is $\frac{3}{4}$ as a decimal?

$3 \div 4 = 0.75$

b) What is 50% as a fraction?

$50 \div 100 = \frac{1}{2}$

2) What is $\frac{4}{5}$ as:

a) a percentage? 80

b) a decimal? 0.8

3) Give the fraction $\frac{3300}{4400}$ in its simplest form.

4) A bank carries out a survey into customer satisfaction. It finds that 2 out of 10 customers are unhappy with the bank's service. What percentage is this?

Comparing Fractions, Percentages and Decimals

You need to be able to compare fractions, percentages and decimals for the test.

Example 1

Which is greater, 0.44 or $\frac{7}{20}$?

You need to work out what $\frac{7}{20}$ is as a decimal.

To convert $\frac{7}{20}$ to a decimal, divide 7 by 20: $7 \div 20 = 0.35$

0.35 is smaller than 0.44, so 0.44 is greater.

Example 2

Niamh is looking at the offers on ready meals in the supermarket:

Sausage Supreme	Spaghetti Bolognese
Normally £2.50	Normally £1.80
Now **Half Price**!	Special offer: **25% off**

Which meal works out cheaper for Niamh to buy?

First work out how much the Sausage Supreme will cost: $\frac{1}{2} \times 2.50 = £1.25$.

Then work out how much the Spaghetti Bolognese will cost:

25% of 1.80 = $\frac{25}{100} \times 1.80 = 0.45$ $1.80 - 0.45 = £1.35$

So the half price Sausage Supreme is cheaper.

Practice Questions

1) Which is greater, 0.04 or $\frac{6}{15}$? ....

2) LEX Comms normally offer broadband at £13.00 per month and line rental at £12.60 per month.   At the moment though, they're offering the two deals below:

    Deal 1: 25% off broadband   Deal 2: a third off line rental

    Which deal would save you the most money each month? Explain your answer.

    ....

    ....

    ....

Proportion

Proportions Compare a Part to the Whole Thing

1) Proportions are a way of showing how much of one part there is compared to the whole thing.

Example

Look at this pattern:

Out of 8 tiles, 2 are white and 6 are blue.

In other words, in every 4 tiles, 1 is white and 3 are blue.

The proportion of white tiles is 1 in every 4.

The proportion of blue tiles is 3 in every 4.

2) Proportions are really another way of writing fractions.

The proportion "1 in every 4" is the same as the fraction $\frac{1}{4}$.

There's more on fractions on pages 11-15.

Practice Questions

1) 60 people have entered the baking contest at a country show. There are different categories for pies, bread, cakes and biscuits.

   a) 15 people enter the biscuit category. What proportion is this of the total entrants?

   ....

   b) 25 people enter the cake category. What proportion is this of the total entrants?

   ....

2) 27 people are waiting at a bus stop. 18 of them are school children. What proportion of the people waiting are school children?

   ....

3) Gareth and his three brothers are the only people in a group of 20 that have birthdays in June. What proportion of the group do they make up?

   ....

Ratios

Ratios Compare One Part to Another Part

Ratios are a way of showing how many things of one type there are compared to another.

Example

Look at this pattern:

There are two white tiles and six blue tiles.

In other words, for every white tile there are three blue tiles.

So the ratio of blue tiles to white tiles is 3:1.

Questions Involving Ratios

To answer a question involving ratios, you usually need to start by working out the value of one part. For example, the cost of one thing or the mass of one part.

You can then use this to answer the question.

Example 1

Orange cordial is diluted by adding 4 parts water to every 1 part of cordial (4:1). How much water should be added to 25 ml of cordial?

1) The amount of cordial used is 1 part, so 1 part = 25 ml.

2) You need 4 parts water to each part cordial so:
   The amount of water needed = amount of cordial × 4
   = 25 ml × 4 = 100 ml

So **100 ml** of water should be added to the cordial.

Example 2

Some jam is made from 1 part sugar to 3 parts fruit (1:3). 500 g of jam is made. How much sugar is used?

1) First work out how many parts there are in total.
   To do this, add up the numbers in the ratio:

   1 + 3 = 4 parts

2) The jam contains 1 part sugar. To work out how many g are in 1 part, divide the total amount of jam by the number of parts:

   500 ÷ 4 = 125 g

So **125 g** of sugar is used.

Example 3

£9000 is split between 3 people in the ratio 2:3:1.
How much money does each person get?

1) First work out how many parts are in the ratio.
   To do this, add up the numbers in the ratio.

$$2 + 3 + 1 = 6$$

2) To find out how much one part is worth, divide 9000 by 6: $9000 \div 6 = 1500$

3) The first person in the ratio gets two parts. To work out how much money
   they get, multiply the value of one part by 2:

$$1500 \times 2 = £3000$$

4) The second person in the ratio gets three parts. To work out how much
   money they get, multiply the value of one part by 3:

$$1500 \times 3 = £4500$$

5) The third person gets 1 part, so they get £1500.

To check your answer, make sure all the parts add up to £9000:
3000 + 4500 + 1500 = £9000.

Working Out Total Amounts

1) You can use ratios to work out total amounts.

2) You need to know the value of one part. (You may have to
   work this out or it might be given to you in the question.)

3) Then work out the total number of parts.

4) You can then multiply the total number of parts by the
   value of one part, to find the total amount.

Example

A jelly is made from one part gelatin and four parts water.
320 g of water is used. How much jelly is made in total?

1) Find the value of one part by dividing the total amount of
   water by the number of parts of water: $320 \div 4 = 80$ g

2) Find the total number of parts by adding up
   the numbers in the ratio: $1 + 4 = 5$

3) Times the total number of parts by the amount
   given for one part: $5 \times 80 = 400$ g

Practice Questions

1) Ollie is making salad dressing. He mixes 1 part vinegar to 2 parts oil.
    Ollie makes 450 ml of salad dressing. How much oil does he use?

    ....

    ....

2) A union votes on whether to go on strike. 120 people vote. The ratio of yes:no votes is 2:3.

    a) How many people vote yes?

        ....

        ....

    b) How many people vote no?

        ....

3) Hamish is making icing. He mixes 1 part icing sugar to 2 parts water.
    He uses 100 g of icing sugar. How much icing will he make?

    ....

    ....

4) Dawn is mixing wallpaper paste. She mixes 1 part glue to 3 parts water.
    Dawn uses 1.5 litres of water. How much wallpaper paste will she make in total?

    ....

    ....

5) George is a sheep farmer. His herd contains Herdwick sheep and Blackface sheep in the
    ratio 3:2. George has 180 Herdwick sheep. How many sheep does he have in total?

    ....

    ....

    ....

Scaling Up and Down

You Can Use Proportion to Scale Up and Down

You can use proportions to scale things up and down.
You usually start by working out the values for one thing.

Example 1

Lucy is making cakes. She finds this recipe ➡

Lucy wants to make 20 cakes.
How much margarine does she need?

Recipe for 12 cakes:
150 g flour
75 g sugar
75 g margarine
3 eggs

1) Start by working out how much margarine
   is needed for 1 cake.

   This recipe is for 12 cakes, so you need
   to divide the weight of the margarine by 12:

   $$75 \div 12 = 6.25 \text{ g}$$

2) To find out how much margarine Lucy needs to make 20 cakes,
   multiply the weight of margarine needed for 1 cake by 20:

   $$6.25 \times 20 = \textbf{125 g}$$

Example 2

6 bags of crisps cost £1.80. How much will 2 bags cost?

1) First, you need to find out how much 1 bag of crisps costs.
   You know that 6 bags cost £1.80, so you need to divide £1.80 by 6.

   $$\text{cost of 1 bag} = 1.80 \div 6 = £0.30$$

2) To work out the cost of 2 bags, times your answer by 2.

   $$0.30 \times 2 = \textbf{£0.60 or 60p}$$

Example 3

Dave is a baker. He bakes 500 biscuits in a 4 hour shift.
How many biscuits can Dave bake in a 6 hour shift?

1) Start by working out how many biscuits Dave bakes in 1 hour.

   He bakes 500 biscuits in 4 hours,
   so you need to divide 500 by 4: $500 \div 4 = 125$ biscuits

2) Multiply your answer by 6 to find out how many biscuits
   Dave can bake in 6 hours: $125 \times 6 = \textbf{750 biscuits}$

Example 4

A breakfast cereal contains 0.4 g of calcium per 100 g. How much calcium does a 35 g serving of the breakfast cereal contain?

1) Start by working out how much calcium is in 1 g of the cereal.

There is 0.4 g of calcium in 100 g of cereal,
so you need to divide 0.4 by 100: $0.4 \div 100 = 0.004$ g

2) Multiply your answer by 35 to find out how much calcium is in 35 g of cereal: $0.004 \times 35 = \textbf{0.14 g}$

Practice Questions

1) Freya is making soup. She needs 500 g of carrots to make 1 litre of soup. How many grams of carrots does she need to make 1.5 litres of soup?

....

....

2) 1000 ml of lemonade contains 250 ml of lemon juice. How much lemon juice does 750 ml of lemonade contain?

....

....

3) Leon runs 10 km in 49 minutes. Assuming he runs at the same speed, how long should it take him to run 18 km?

....

....

4) Sharon is making greetings cards. Each card takes her twenty minutes to make. How many can she complete in two and a half hours?

....

....

Formulas in Words

A Formula is a Type of Rule

1) A formula is a rule for working out an amount.

2) Formulas can be written in words. Sometimes, it can be tricky to spot the formula.

Example

Mike packs 40 boxes an hour. How many boxes can he pack in 6.5 hours?

You're told that: "Mike packs 40 boxes an hour." This is a formula. You can use it to work out how many boxes Mike can pack in a given number of hours.

1) The calculation you need to do here is:

Number of boxes = 40 × number of hours

2) You've been asked how many boxes Mike can pack in 6.5 hours, so put '6.5' into the calculation in place of 'number of hours':

Number of boxes = 40 × 6.5 = 260

You can use the same formula to work out how many boxes Mike can pack in any number of hours.

Formulas Can Have More Than One Step

Some formulas have two steps in them. You need to be able to use two-step formulas.

Example

Owen has moved into a new house. The telephone company will charge him £110 to connect his phone line, then line rental at £11.50 per month. How much will Owen's phone line have cost him after 12 months?

The formula here is "£11.50 per month, plus £110".

1) Work out the calculation you need to do:

Step 1 = 11.50 × number of months

Step 2 = + 110

There's more on brackets on page 6.

Cost of phone line = (11.50 × number of months) + 110

2) Then just stick the right numbers in.
   In this case it's '12' in place of 'number of months':

(11.50 × 12) + 110 = £248

Practice Questions

1) Dan is getting some furniture delivered. Delivery costs £5 per item, plus £20 to assemble all the items. How much will it cost Dan to get 4 items of furniture delivered and assembled?

....

....

2) Chrissie needs a wallpaper stripper. It costs £10 a day to hire, plus a deposit of £40. How much will it cost Chrissie to hire the wallpaper stripper for 3 days (including the deposit)?

....

....

3) Angela is leaving her car parked at the airport whilst she goes away on business for 5 days. It costs £11.50 per day to park there and there is a one-off charge of £10.
How much will it cost Angela to park for 5 days?

....

....

4) Shabnam is a babysitter. She charges £5.00 an hour before midnight and £6.50 an hour after midnight. How much will Shabnam earn babysitting from 8 pm to 2 am?

....

....

....

5) Josie takes a taxi when she travels between her house and town.
The journey from her house to town (or the other way around) usually costs £8.
If she travels after 11 pm the journey costs £12.

In one week Josie travelled to town and back four times. All the trips to town were before 11 pm. One journey back was after 11 pm. How much did she spend on taxis?

....

....

....

More Formulas

Formulas Can be Shown Using Letters

You might be given a formula made up of letters. Each letter represents something.

Example

To work out speed you divide distance by time.

As words, this can be written as:

speed = distance ÷ time

The formula can be shortened by using letters instead of full words.

s = d ÷ t

s represents speed   d represents distance   t represents time

Putting Numbers into Formulas

You can substitute numbers into a formula that is written as letters.

Example 1

s = d ÷ t   s represents speed
d represents distance
t represents time

A bus travels 100 metres in 8 seconds. Work out the speed it was travelling.

1) Start by working out what letters you have values for and what they are.

You're told that the bus travels a distance of 100 m, so d = 100 m.
You're told the bus travels for 8 seconds, so t = 8 s.

2) You can substitute these numbers into the formula:

s = d ÷ t

s = 100 ÷ 8

s = 12.5 metres per second

The units are metres per second as you're dividing a distance in metres by a time in seconds

So the bus is travelling at **12.5 metres per second**.

Example 2

GlobalPhone mobile phone deals are worked out using the formula below.

$$cost = m(5n + 1000)$$

cost = price in pence, m = number of months,
n = number of free text messages per month.

Jack wants a 12 month deal, with 500 free texts per month.
How much will this cost?

1) Start by writing the formula out in full.
   Times (×) signs are sometimes left out of formulas to simplify them.

   So... $5n = 5 × n$ and $m(5n + 1000) = m × (5n + 1000)$

   So the formula can be written as: $cost = m × (5 × n + 1000)$

2) Work out what values the letters have:

   Jack wants a 12 month contract, so m = 12.
   He wants 500 free texts, so n = 500.

3) Substitute these numbers into the formula:

$$cost = 12 × (5 × 500 + 1000)$$
$$cost = 12 × (3500)$$
$$cost = 42\ 000\ p$$

So it will cost **42 000p** or **£420**.

Example 3

Temperature can be measured in degrees Celsius (°C) or degrees Fahrenheit (°F). The formula: $F = \frac{9}{5}C + 32$ can be used to swap between the two.

C represents Celsius and F represents Fahrenheit.

If the temperature is 15 °C, what is the temperature in Fahrenheit?

1) Write out the formula in full: $F = \frac{9}{5} × C + 32$

2) Put numbers in place of any letters you know.
   Here you're told that C = 15: $F = \frac{9}{5} × 15 + 32$

3) Work it out in stages.
   Write down values for each bit as you go along: $F = 27 + 32$
                                                         $F = 59$

So the temperature is **59 °F**.

Practice Questions

1) Jim uses the formula below to work out how many fence posts he needs.

$$n = p + 1$$

Where n = number of fence posts and p = number of fence panels.

a) Jim's front garden fence will have 6 panels. How many fence posts does he need?

....

b) Jim's back garden fence will have 13 panels.
How many fence posts does he need for the back garden?

....

2) A teacher is organising a school trip. The formula $s = c \div 20$ is used to work out the number of staff needed on the trip. s represents the number of staff needed and c represents the number of children on the trip. If 80 children are on the trip, how many staff are needed?

....

....

3) The formula on the right is used to find the cost in pounds, (including a deposit), of hiring some bikes. Jill wants to hire 4 bikes for 5 hours. How much will this cost?

> Cost = b(10n + 30)
> b = number of bikes
> n = number of hours

....

....

....

You May Need to Rearrange Formulas

Sometimes you'll need to rearrange a formula.

Example

A car travelling at 30 m/s travels 300 metres.
Calculate the time this takes.

You know speed and distance, and you need to work out the time. But the formula you've got is $s = d \div t$.

So you need to rearrange it so you have t = instead of s =

> $s = d \div t$
>
> s = speed,
> d = distance,
> t = time.

How to Rearrange Formulas

Find the letter you need to work out the value of — it's this letter you need to get on its own.

Then rearrange the formula by adding, subtracting, multiplying or dividing letters.

But you can't just move the letters around however you'd like. There are rules to follow:

1) You use multiplications to remove divisions.

2) You use divisions to remove multiplications.

3) You use adding to remove subtractions.

4) You use subtractions to remove additions.

5) If you add, subtract, multiply or divide one side of the formula you need to do exactly the same to the other side.

Example 1

The formula below can be used to work out how many students are in a class.

$$n = m + w$$

Where n = total number of students, m = number of men, w = number of women.

There are 31 students in a class, 16 are women. How many are men?

1) You need to get m on its own, so you need to move the + w.

2) Write out the original equation. $\longrightarrow$ $n = m + w$
Subtract w from both sides. $\longrightarrow$ $n - w = m + w - w$
The + w and − w cancel each other out. $\longrightarrow$ $n - w = m$

3) Put the numbers you know into the rearranged formula:

The left and right side have just been swapped $\longrightarrow$ $m = n - w$
around so it's a bit easier to see m on its own. $\quad m = 31 - 16$
$$m = \mathbf{15}$$

Example 2

A car drives for 15 seconds at a speed of 30 m/s.
Calculate the distance it travels in this time.

$s = d \div t$

s = speed,
d = distance,
t = time.

1) You need to get d on its own, so you need to move the ÷ t.

2) Write out the original equation. $\longrightarrow$ $s = d \div t$
Multiply both sides by t. $\longrightarrow$ $t \times s = d \div t \times t$
÷ t and × t cancel each other out. $\longrightarrow$ $t \times s = d$

3) Put the numbers you know into the rearranged formula.
$d = s \times t$
$d = 30 \times 15$
$$d = \mathbf{450\ m}$$ $\longleftarrow$ Don't forget your units.

Example 3

The formula below is used to work out the cost of hiring some boats.

Cost in pounds = b(5h + d)
b = number of boats, h = number of hours, d = deposit per boat

Faheem has paid £60 to hire 3 boats for 1 hour. How much was the deposit?

1) You need to get d on its own so you need to move b and 5h to the other side.

2) Cost = b(5h + d) is the same as Cost = b × (5h + d).

3) Divide both sides by b. ➡ Cost ÷ b = b × (5h + d) ÷ b
   Cost ÷ b = (5h + d)

4) Subtract 5h from both sides. ➡ (Cost ÷ b) − 5h = 5h + d − 5h
   (Cost ÷ b) − 5h = d

5) Put in the numbers you know and find the value of d.
   d = (60 ÷ 3) − (5 × 1) ⬅ 5h is the same as 5 × h.
   d = 20 − 5 = £15

6) This is the deposit per boat, so multiply it by 3.
   Total deposit = 3 × 15 = **£45**

Practice Questions

1) A distance in miles (M) can be changed into kilometres (K) using the formula below:
$$M = \frac{5}{8}K$$
If a van travels 3.75 miles, how far has it travelled in kilometres?

....

....

2) The length of material needed to make a skirt can be worked out using the formula
m = 1.5w + 5. m = length of material (in cm) and w = waist measurement (in cm). If a piece of cloth is 95 cm long what is the maximum waist measurement a skirt could have?

....

....

....

Units

All Measures Have Units

1) Almost everything that you measure has units. For example, metres (m) or grams (g).

2) They're really important. For example, you can't just say that a distance is 4 — you need to know if it's 4 miles, 4 metres, 4 kilometres, etc.

Units of Length

1) Length is how long something is. Some common units for length are millimetres (mm), centimetres (cm), metres (m) and kilometres (km).

2) Here's how some of these units are related: ⟶

3) Sometimes you might need to change something from one unit to another.

Length
1 cm = 10 mm
1 m = 100 cm
1 km = 1000 m

4) To switch between mm, cm, m and km you can multiply or divide by 10, 100, or 1000.

To go from mm to cm, divide by 10.	To go from cm to mm, multiply by 10.
To go from cm to m, divide by 100.	To go from m to cm, multiply by 100.
To go from m to km, divide by 1000.	To go from km to m, multiply by 1000.

Example 1

What is 2.7 km in m?

Answer: You're going from km to m, so multiply by 1000.

$$2.7 \text{ km} \times 1000 = 2700 \text{ m}$$

Example 2

What is 1570 mm in m?

Answer: First change from mm to cm, by dividing by 10.

$$1570 \div 10 = 157 \text{ cm}$$

Then change from cm to m, by dividing by 100.

$$157 \div 100 = 1.57 \text{ m}$$

Units of Weight

1) Weight is how heavy something is. Grams (g) and kilograms (kg) are common units for weight.

Weight
1 kg = 1000 g

2) Here's how to change between g and kg...

To go from g to kg, divide by 1000.

To go from kg to g, multiply by 1000.

Example

How many grams are there in 0.7 kg?

Answer: You're going from kg to g so multiply by 1000.

0.7 kg × 1000 = 700 g

Units of Capacity

1) Capacity is how much something will hold. Common units are millilitres (ml), centilitres (cl) and litres (L) .

2) To change between ml, cl and L you can multiply or divide by 10 or 100.

Capacity
1 cl = 10 ml
1 L = 100 cl

To go from ml to cl, divide by 10.

To go from cl to L, divide by 100.

To go from cl to ml, multiply by 10.

To go from L to cl, multiply by 100.

Example

How many millilitres are in 0.34 L?

Answer: First change from L to cl, by multiplying by 100.

0.34 L × 100 = 34 cl

Then change from cl to ml, by multiplying by 10.

34 × 10 = 340 ml

Converting Between Other Units

1) Sometimes you can't change from one unit to another by multiplying or dividing by 10, 100 or 1000.

2) You may have to multiply or divide by a different number — the number you need will be in the question. You need to follow two rules:

   - Write out the information in the question, with an equals sign (=) in the middle.

   - Whatever you do to the number on the left-hand side of the '=', you need to do the same to the number on the right-hand side. (And vice versa.)

Example

1 kg is equal to 2.2 lbs (pounds). How many lbs are in 4 kg?

1) Write out the information that you know: 1 kg = 2.2 lbs

2) To go from 1 kg to 4 kg you need to multiply by 4. So to find out how many lbs are in 4 kg you also need to multiply the number of pounds by 4:

$$1 \text{ kg} = 2.2 \text{ lbs} \longrightarrow 1 \text{ kg} \times 4 = 2.2 \text{ lbs} \times 4 \longrightarrow 4 \text{ kg} = \textbf{8.8 lbs}$$

Multiply both sides by 4   Work out the answer

3) Sometimes you may need to do the calculation in two bits. You may have to divide first, to find out the value of one unit, and then multiply to find the value of the number of units you're asked for.

Example

1 oz (ounce) is equal to 28 g. How many oz are in 42 g?

1) Write out the information that you know: 28 g = 1 oz

2) First, find out how many oz are in 1 g by dividing both sides by the number of g in 1 oz — which is 28.

$$28 \text{ g} = 1 \text{ oz} \longrightarrow \frac{28}{28} \text{ g} = \frac{1}{28} \text{ oz} \longrightarrow 1 \text{ g} = \frac{1}{28} \text{ oz}$$

Divide both sides by 28   This gives you the number of oz in 1 g

3) Then work out how many oz are in 42 g by multiplying both sides by 42.

$$1 \text{ g} = \frac{1}{28} \text{ oz} \longrightarrow 1 \text{ g} \times 42 = \frac{1}{28} \text{ oz} \times 42 \longrightarrow 42 \text{ g} = \textbf{1.5 oz}$$

Multiply both sides by 42   Work out the answer

Just remember, whatever you do to the number on the left-hand side,
you need to do the same to the number on the right-hand side.

Practice Questions

1) How many m are in 7.5 km?

....

2) What is 6400 g in kg?

....

3) What is 560 millilitres in litres?

....

4) 1 kg is equal to 2.2 lbs. How many lbs are in 15 kg?

....

5) 1 km = 0.62 miles. Sally has cycled 10 km. How far has she cycled in miles?

....

6) 1 British pound (£) is the same value as 1.5 Australian dollars ($).
   Deepika paid $450 for a flight. How much is this in pounds?

....

....

7) 1 litre = 35 fluid ounces (fl. oz). Joe needs 7 fl. oz of milk for a recipe.

   a)   How many litres of milk does Joe need?

   ....

   b)   How many millilitres of milk does Joe need?

   ....

8) 1 foot = 12 inches. 1 inch = 2.54 cm.
   Chris is 6 feet and 3 inches tall. How tall is he in cm?

....

....

....

Length and Perimeter

Finding the Perimeter of a Shape

1) The perimeter is the distance around the outside of a shape.

2) To find a perimeter, you add up the lengths of all the sides.

Example

Find the perimeter of the shape on the right.

Just add up the lengths of all the
sides — be careful not to miss any.

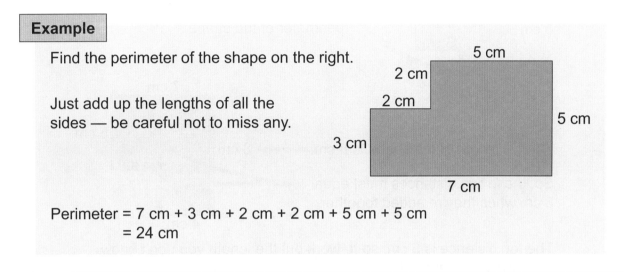

Perimeter = 7 cm + 3 cm + 2 cm + 2 cm + 5 cm + 5 cm
= 24 cm

Working Out the Lengths of Sides of Rectangles

If you're only given the lengths of some of the sides, you'll have to work out the rest
before you can calculate the perimeter. Sometimes this is fairly simple.

Example

This rectangle has 4 sides, but you're
only given the lengths of 2 of them.

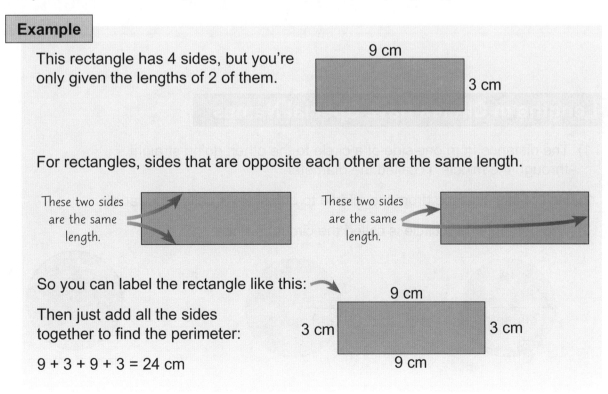

For rectangles, sides that are opposite each other are the same length.

These two sides
are the same
length.

These two sides
are the same
length.

So you can label the rectangle like this:

Then just add all the sides
together to find the perimeter:

9 + 3 + 9 + 3 = 24 cm

Working Out the Length of Unknown Sides of Other Shapes

It's a bit harder to find the lengths of unknown sides if you're not dealing with rectangles.

What is the perimeter of the shape below?

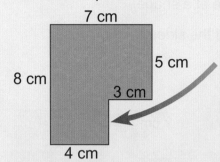

You need to work out the length of this side before you can find the perimeter of the shape.

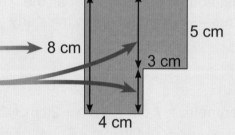

The full length of the shape is 8 cm. ➡ 8 cm

So, these two distances must equal 8 cm when they're added together.

The top distance is 5 cm, so to work out the length you don't know, take away 5 cm from 8 cm:

$$8 \text{ cm} - 5 \text{ cm} = 3 \text{ cm}$$

The unknown side must be 3 cm long.

Now you can just work out the perimeter as usual...

Perimeter = 8 cm + 7 cm + 5 cm + 3 cm + 3 cm + 4 cm = 30 cm

Lengths in Circles Have Special Names

1) The distance from one side of a circle to the other, going straight through the middle, is called the diameter.

2) Half of this distance (from the middle to one side) is called the radius.

3) The perimeter of a circle is called the circumference.

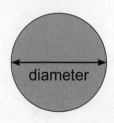

diameter

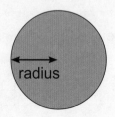

radius

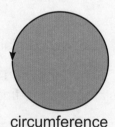

circumference

Practice Questions

1) Work out the perimeters of the shapes below.

   a)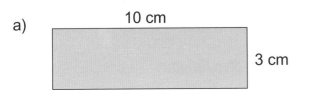

   b)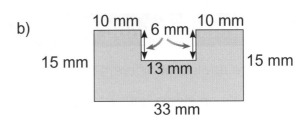

   ....

2) Look at the circle on the right.

   a) What is the diameter of the circle?

   ....

   b) What is the radius of the circle?

   ....

   c) What name is given to the perimeter of a circle?

   ....

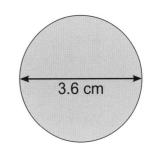

3) Look at the shape on the right.

   a) What is the length of the side labelled A?

   ....

   b) What is the length of the side labelled B?

   ....

   c) What is the perimeter of the shape?

   ....

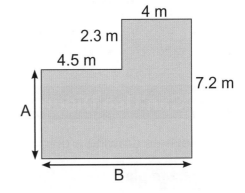

4) What is the perimeter of the shape below?

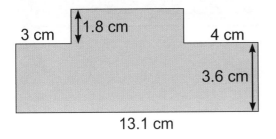

   ....

   ....

   ....

   ....

Working with Lengths

Questions Involving Length

1) There are lots of different types of questions that involve length.

2) There's no single right way to answer them, just use the information that you're given and work through it in a sensible way.

Example

Ruaridh is tiling his kitchen floor. The floor is 2.8 m wide and 4.4 m long.
The tiles are 40 cm long and 40 cm wide. How many tiles will Ruaridh need?

1) Start by changing the sizes of the tiles from cm to m, so that all the lengths are in the same units:

$$40 \text{ cm} \div 100 = 0.4 \text{ m} \qquad \text{Each tile is 0.4 m by 0.4 m.}$$

2) Work out how many tiles he needs to make one row across the kitchen:

$$4.4 \text{ m} \div 0.4 \text{ m} = 11 \text{ tiles}$$

3) Work out how many rows are needed:

$$2.8 \text{ m} \div 0.4 \text{ m} = 7 \text{ rows}$$

4) Calculate the total number of tiles.
He'll need 7 rows of 11 tiles:

$$7 \times 11 = \textbf{77 tiles}$$

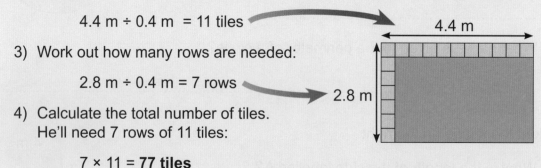

You Can Use Diagrams to Help Answer Questions

Sometimes drawing a diagram can help you to answer a question involving length.

Example

A flower bed is 1.3 m long. Anne has some plants that need to be planted 20 cm apart. How many plants can she fit in one row?

Convert the length of the flower bed to cm, so all lengths are in the same units — 1.3 m × 100 = 130 cm. The flower bed is 130 cm long.

Choose a sensible distance in from the edge of the bed to plant the first plant.

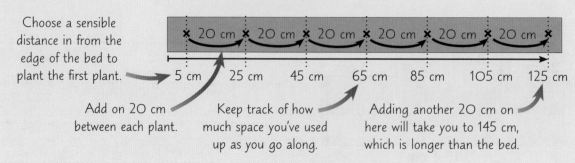

Add on 20 cm between each plant.

Keep track of how much space you've used up as you go along.

Adding another 20 cm on here will take you to 145 cm, which is longer than the bed.

So Anne can fit **7 plants** in one row in the flower bed.

Questions Involving Different Shapes and Lengths

Sometimes you'll have to deal with different shapes and lengths in one question.

Example

Alan wants to build a feature wall at the end of his patio. The two types of bricks he has and the pattern he wants to arrange them in are shown below. He needs to leave a 1 cm gap between each of the bricks. Gaps at the ends that aren't big enough for whole bricks will be filled with concrete.

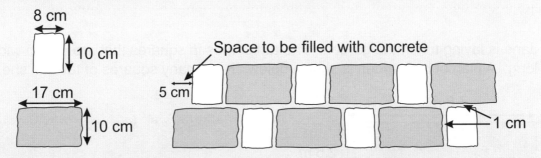

The wall needs to be 325 cm across and will be two rows high. How many of each type of brick will he need?

1) Group the lengths together into a section of wall that will repeat over and over. For example...

   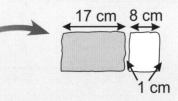

   1 large brick, a gap, 1 small brick and another gap has a total length of: 17 + 1 + 8 + 1 = 27 cm

2) The wall needs to be 325 cm.

   325 ÷ 27 = 12.037...   So the section of wall will repeat 12 times in one row.

   Work out the exact length of the wall if this section is repeated 12 times:

   12 × 27 = 324 cm   So there will be a 1 cm space at the end.
                         No brick will fit there, so it will be filled with concrete.

3) The second row of the wall starts 5 cm further in than the first row.
   So the amount of space left to fill with bricks is: 325 – 5 = 320 cm

   320 ÷ 27 = 11.85...   So the section of wall will repeat 11 times.

   The exact length of the wall if this section is repeated 11 times is:

   11 × 27 = 297 cm   So there will be 320 – 297 = 23 cm left over.
                         One more large brick could fit in this space.

4) Work out the total number of bricks.

   1st row: 12 large bricks and 12 small bricks.

   2nd row: 12 large bricks and 11 small bricks.

   Total: 24 large bricks, 23 small bricks.

Practice Questions

1) Asif is wallpapering a wall in his dining room. The wall is 3.4 m wide. The wallpaper strips are 40 cm wide. How many strips will Asif need to buy to cover the width of the wall?

....

....

....

2) Jane is laying turf in the garden. The turf comes in squares that are 50 cm wide and 50 cm long. A plan of her garden is shown below. How many squares of turf will she need?

....

....

....

....

....

....

3) Sarah is setting up an exam hall with rows of desks facing the front of the hall. The hall is 12 m wide and 15 m long. Each desk is 70 cm wide and 50 cm long. She needs to leave a 1 m gap between each desk. Starting in a corner, how many desks can she fit into the hall?

....

....

....

....

Areas of Squares and Rectangles

You Can Find the Area of Shapes by Multiplying

1) Area is how much surface a shape covers.

2) You can work out the area of squares and rectangles by multiplying the lengths of the sides together.

Example 1

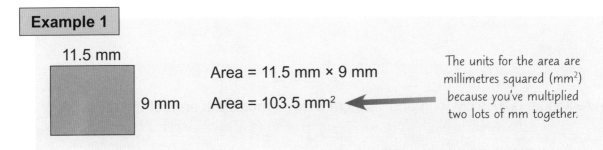

11.5 mm

9 mm

Area = 11.5 mm × 9 mm

Area = 103.5 mm²

The units for the area are millimetres squared (mm²) because you've multiplied two lots of mm together.

Example 2

Lily's lawn is 12.6 m long and 8.55 m wide. What is the area of the lawn?

Answer: 12.6 × 8.55 = 107.73 m²

Sometimes You Need to Split Shapes Up to Find the Area

It's a bit trickier to find the area of a shape that isn't a rectangle...

...but you can sometimes do it by splitting the shape up into rectangles.

Example

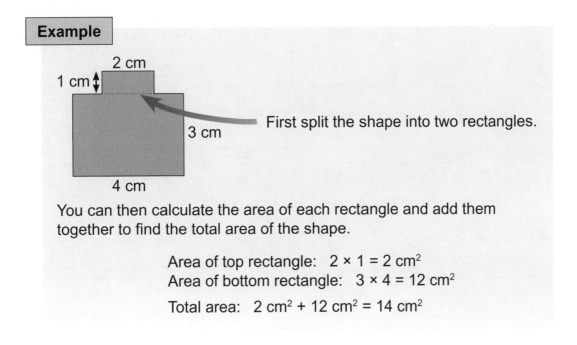

2 cm

1 cm

3 cm

4 cm

First split the shape into two rectangles.

You can then calculate the area of each rectangle and add them together to find the total area of the shape.

Area of top rectangle: 2 × 1 = 2 cm²
Area of bottom rectangle: 3 × 4 = 12 cm²

Total area: 2 cm² + 12 cm² = 14 cm²

Practice Questions

1) Work out the area of the shapes below.

a)

2 cm

2 cm

b)

10.7 m

1.1 m

....

....

2) A rectangle is 37.5 cm long and 14.0 cm wide. What is the area of the rectangle?

....

3) Each side of a square is 0.9 m long. What is the area of the square?

....

4) Find the area of the shapes below.

a)

4.4 cm

3.2 cm

6 cm

3.7 cm

2.8 cm

8.1 cm

b)

13 cm

11 cm

11 cm

5 cm

3 cm   3 cm

....

....

....

....

....

....

Areas of Triangles and Circles

You Can Work Out The Area of a Triangle by Multiplying

1) To work out the area of a triangle you need to multiply the length of its base by its height, and then divide by two.

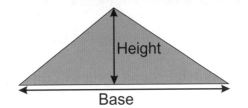

2) This can be written as a formula:

Area of triangle = base × height ÷ 2

Examples

Area of triangle = base × height ÷ 2

    = 7.4 cm × 3 cm ÷ 2

    = 11.1 cm²

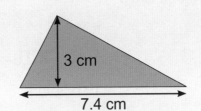

Area of triangle = base × height ÷ 2

    = 9 cm × 11 cm ÷ 2

    = 49.5 cm²

This is the height of the triangle — not the side labelled 11.9 cm.

To Calculate the Area of a Circle You Need to Use Pi (π)

There's also a formula for working out the area of a circle.

Area of circle = π × radius²

The little '2' means the radius is squared. This means you multiply it by itself. So $r^2 = r \times r$.

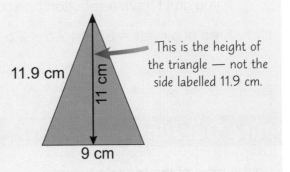

radius of a circle

The symbol π (called "pi") is just a very long number (3.14159...).

If you have a π button on your calculator you can use it in calculations.

If you don't have a π button, just type in 3.14 instead of π.

Pi is actually said like "pie".

More on Calculating the Area of a Circle

1) If you're asked to work out the area of a circle in your test, you'll be given the formula.

2) It may look like the formula on the previous page.

Area of circle = π × radius²

3) Or it could be written like this:

Area of circle = π × r²   or this...   Area of circle = πr²

4) They all mean the same thing though — just π (or 3.14) multiplied by the radius squared.

5) So all you have to do is put the radius of the circle into the formula, and work it out.

Example

Area of a circle = π × r²

$= π × 2.5^2$

$= π × 2.5 × 2.5$

= 19.63495...

= 19.63 cm²

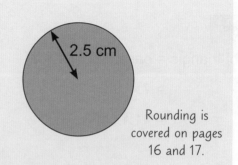
2.5 cm

Rounding is covered on pages 16 and 17.

If you don't have a π button on your calculator you'll need to do...

Area of a circle = 3.14 × 2.5 × 2.5 = 19.625 cm² instead.

Practice Questions

1) Find the area of the triangle below.

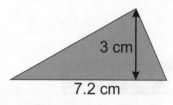
3 cm

7.2 cm

....

....

....

2) Find the area of the circle below. Use the formula, area = π × r².

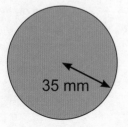
35 mm

....

....

....

More on Area

Using Areas in Calculations

Sometimes you'll need to work out an area as part of a bigger calculation.

Example 1

Joel is painting the side of a house, shown on the right.
A tin of paint will cover 20 m².
Joel needs to give the wall 2 coats of paint.

How many tins of paint does he need to buy?

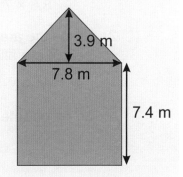

1) If you split the house into a triangle and a rectangle,
   you can work out the area of the side of the house.

   Area of triangle = base × height ÷ 2

   $\qquad$ = 7.8 × 3.9 ÷ 2

   $\qquad$ = 15.21 m²

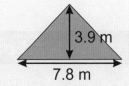

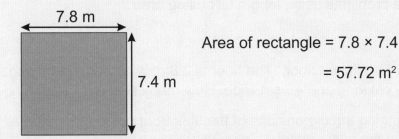

Area of rectangle = 7.8 × 7.4

$\qquad$ = 57.72 m²

2) Then add the two areas together to find the total area of the side of the house:

   15.21 m² + 57.72 m² = 72.93 m²

3) Joel needs to paint this area twice, so the total area that he will paint is:

   72.93 × 2 = 145.86 m²

4) Now work out how many tins of paint Joel needs to paint this area.
   To do this, divide the total area he will paint by the area that one tin will cover:

   145.86 m² ÷ 20 m² = 7.293... tins

Joel can't buy 7.293 tins of paint, so he'll have to buy **8 tins**.

Example 2

Francine runs a slimming group.
The hall where the group meets is 8.6 m long and 7.2 m wide.
Health and Safety rules state for each person in the hall there must be 1.5 m²
of floor space. How many people (including Fran) can go to the group?

1) Work out the area of the hall.

   $8.6 \times 7.2 = 61.92$ m²

2) Divide the area of the hall by 1.5 m² to find out how many
    people are allowed in the hall at a time.

   $61.92 \div 1.5 = 41.28$

   So **41 people** can go to the group.

You Can Use Area Instead of Using Length

Some problems can be answered in lots of different ways. For example, you can work
out the answer to some problems using length OR using area.

Example

Ruaridh is tiling his kitchen floor. The floor is 2.8 m wide and 4.4 m long.
The tiles are 40 cm long and 40 cm wide. How many tiles will Ruaridh need?

1) Start by changing the dimensions of the tiles from cm to m, so that all the
    lengths are in the same units:

   40 cm $\div 100 = 0.4$ m   Each tile is 0.4 m by 0.4 m.

2) You need to work out how many tiles will fit into the area of the floor.
    So calculate the area of the floor: $2.8 \times 4.4 = 12.32$ m²

3) Then calculate the area of one tile: $0.4 \times 0.4 = 0.16$ m²

4) Now divide the area of the floor by the area of one tile:

   $12.32 \div 0.16 =$ **77 tiles**

You could also answer this question using length — see page 46.

Surface Area is the Total Area of the Sides of a Shape

1) Sometimes you might need to work out the surface area of a shape.

2) This is just the areas of all the sides of the shape added together.

Example

The box below has two sides with an area of 91 cm², two sides with an area of 70 cm², and two sides with an area of 32.5 cm².

So the surface area of the shape is:

91 + 91 + 70 + 70 + 32.5 + 32.5 = 387 cm²

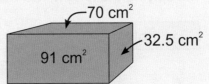

Practice Questions

1) The base of the pyramid on the right has an area of 25 cm².
   The four other sides have an area of 15 cm² each.
   What is the surface area of the pyramid?

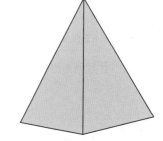

   ....

   ....

2) Carlos is laying concrete to make the floors of two rooms. The dimensions of the rooms are shown below. He needs to use 0.1 m³ of concrete to make 1 m² of floor. The concrete will cost £65 per m³. How much will it cost to buy enough concrete for the floors?

7 m 3 m   6 m 2 m

....

....

....

....

....

Volume

You Can Calculate the Volume of a Shape by Multiplying

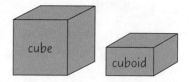

1) Volume is how much space something takes up.

2) You can work out the volume of cubes and cuboids by multiplying the length, the width and the height together.

Example

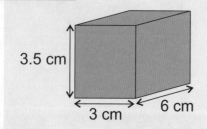

Length = 6 cm   Width = 3 cm   Height = 3.5 cm

Volume = length × width × height

= 6 cm × 3 cm × 3.5 cm

= 63 cm³

The units are cm³ in this example, because you've multiplied three lots of cm together.

If the sides were measured in m, the units for volume would be m³.

Using Volumes in Calculations

You may have to work out volume as part of a bigger calculation.

Example

Iain's fish tank is 0.9 m long, 0.3 m wide and 0.4 m high.
He is filling it with water using a container that has a volume of 3000 cm³.

How many times will he need to empty the container into the tank to fill the tank?

1) Convert the sizes of Iain's fish tank into cm so that all measurements are in the same units: 0.9 m = 90 cm, 0.3 m = 30 cm and 0.4 m = 40 cm.

2) Calculate the volume of the tank. ⟶ 90 × 30 × 40 = 108 000 cm³

3) Calculate how many times the volume of the container will go into the volume of the tank. ⟶ 108 000 ÷ 3000 = 36

So Iain will need to empty the container **36 times** to fill the tank.

Practice Questions

1) Calculate the volume of the shapes below.

a)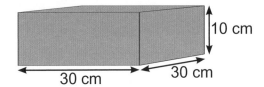
10 cm
30 cm   30 cm

....

b)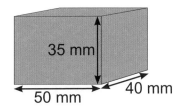
35 mm
50 mm   40 mm

....

2) Sarah has a suitcase that is 1.2 m long, 0.7 m wide and 20 cm deep.
What is the volume of the suitcase?

....

....

3) George is buying gravel to put on his driveway. The driveway is shown below.
He needs the gravel to be 2 cm deep. He can buy gravel in bags that weigh
1 tonne, and cover 1 000 000 cm³. How many bags will he need to buy?

12.2 m

3.0 m

....

....

....

....

....

Money

Pounds and Pence

1) If you get a question on money, the units will probably be pounds (£) or pence (p).

2) You need to be able to switch between using pounds and using pence.

> To go from pounds to pence, multiply by 100.
>
> To go from pence to pounds, divide by 100.

Examples

What is £11.25 in pence?

Answer: You're going from pounds to pence, so multiply by 100.

$$£11.25 × 100 = 1125p$$

What is 37p in pounds?

Answer: You're going from pence to pounds, so divide by 100.

$$37p ÷ 100 = £0.37$$

Use Pounds OR Pence in Calculations — Not Both

1) You may get a question that uses pounds and pence.

2) If you do, you'll need to change the units so that they're all in pounds or all in pence.

Example

Callum buys fish and chips for £5.25, a carton of gravy for 60p and a cup of tea for 75p. How much does he need to pay in total?

1) Change the carton of gravy and cup of tea from pence to pounds.

$$60p ÷ 100 = £0.60$$

$$75p ÷ 100 = £0.75$$

2) All the prices are in the same units now (£), so just add them up.

$$£5.25 + £0.60 + £0.75 = £6.60$$

3) If the question tells you what units to give your answer in then make sure you use those. If it doesn't, you can change everything into pounds or into pence.

Calculate the Price Per Item to Work Out Value For Money

1) If you're buying a pack of something, you can work out how much you're paying for each item.

Price per item = total price ÷ number of items

2) You can then compare the price per item for that pack with other packs.

Example

A shop sells crisps in multipacks of 6 or 12.
The 6-pack costs £1.68. The 12-pack costs £3.00.

6-pack: Price per bag = £1.68 ÷ 6 = £0.28

Price per bag = total price ÷ number of bags

12-pack: Price per bag = £3.00 ÷ 12 = £0.25

The 12-pack costs less per bag, so it's better value than the 6-pack.

You Can Also Calculate the Price Per Gram

You can also compare costs by looking at how much you'd pay per unit weight of something. For example, how much you'd pay per gram, or per kilogram.

Price per gram = total price ÷ number of grams

Example

An 800 g bag of muesli costs £2.00. A 500 g bag of muesli costs £1.50.

800 g bag: Price per gram = £2.00 ÷ 800 = £0.0025

500 g bag: Price per gram = £1.50 ÷ 500 = £0.003

The prices per gram are very small numbers. It's easier to compare them when the units are pence, so convert the price per gram from pounds to pence.

800 g bag: Price per gram = 200p ÷ 800 = 0.25p

500 g bag: Price per gram = 150p ÷ 500 = 0.30p

The 800 g bag costs less per gram, so it's better value than the 500 g bag.

If you needed to work out the price per kilogram or the price per ounce, for example, you'd do it in exactly the same way — just swap grams for the units you're using.

Practice Questions

1) a) What is £16.42 in pence?   b) What is 210p in pounds?

   ....

2) A pet shop sells a 6-can multipack of dog food for £3.18 and a 12-can multipack for £6.24. Which multipack is the best value for money?

   ....

   ....

3) Michelle buys a 14 g jar of herbs for £0.95. Her friend Zoe buys a 7 g jar for £0.60. Who has got the best value?

   ....

   ....

Work Out the Value of Offers to Find the Best Deal

To find the best deal you need to work out how much you'd pay with each offer, or which offer takes the most off the total price.

Example

Malcolm wants to hire a van for two days from Hire-a-van or Speedy Hire.

Hire-a-van — £65 per day with 15% off the total price for bookings of more than one day.

Speedy Hire — £63 per day.

Malcolm has a £10 off voucher he could use with Speedy Hire.

Which company should Malcolm use to get the best deal?

Hire-a-van ➝ Cost of two days' hire = £65 × 2 = £130
Discount for booking two days = 15 ÷ 100 × £130 = £19.50
Total cost = £130 − £19.50 = £110.50

Speedy Hire ➝ Cost of two days' hire = £63 × 2 = £126
Voucher discount = £10
Total cost = £126 − £10 = £116

So Malcolm will get the best deal by hiring a van from Hire-a-van.

Profit is the Amount of Money Made

Profit is the difference between the cost of making something and the price it's sold for.

Profit = selling price – cost of making it

Example

Geoff makes wooden benches. Each bench costs him £34 to make and he sells them for £75. How much profit does Geoff make on each bench?

Profit = £75 – £34 = £41

Geoff makes £41 on each bench he sells.

If something costs more to make than it sells for, the profit will be a negative number — this is called a loss.

Percentage Profit Compares Money Made to Money Spent

You could be asked to work out the percentage profit made on an item. To work this out you need to calculate the profit and then work out what this is as a percentage of the cost of making it.

Example 1

Chloe makes and sells stuffed animal toys. The cost of making her last toy was £40. The toy sold on an auction website for £52.
How much profit did she make?

1) Work out the profit. ⟶ Profit = selling price – cost of making
$$= £52 - £40 = £12$$

2) Work out the percentage profit. ⟶ % profit = $\frac{12}{40} \times 100 = 30\%$

So Chloe made a 30% profit on the toy.

Example 2

For her next toy, Chloe want to make a 40% profit.
The cost of making the toy is £25.
What price does the toy need to sell for to make 40% profit?

1) Work out 40% of the costs. ⟶ $\frac{40}{100} \times £25 = £10$

2) Add this 40% to the costs. ⟶ £25 + £10 = £35

So Chloe needs to charge £35 to make 40% profit on this toy.

Practice Questions

1) Gillian is buying a new carpet that she would like fitting in her lounge.
    The carpet showroom offers Gillian free fitting or 20% off her total bill.

    The cost of the carpet is £396.50
    The cost of fitting is £120.00

    Which offer will save Gillian the most money?

    ....

    ....

    ....

2) Josh buys 2 bottles of lemonade that are on a buy one get one half price offer.
    They normally cost £0.90 each. How much does Josh save with the offer?

    ....

    ....

3) Dafydd sells DVDs on a market stall.
    He buys the DVDs for £2.60 and sells them on for £3.90.

    a) How much profit does he make on each DVD?

    ....

    b) What is Dafydd's percentage profit on each DVD?

    ....

    ....

4) Luke makes fruit cakes for a stall at a village fete. It costs Luke £1.80 for the ingredients for
    each cake. If he wants to make 35% profit on each cake, how much money should Luke be
    charging for each cake?

    ....

    ....

    ....

    ....

    ....

Time

The 12-Hour Clock and the 24-Hour Clock

1) You can give the time using the 12-hour clock or the 24-hour clock.

2) The 24-hour clock goes from 00:00 (midnight) to 23:59 (one minute before the next midnight).

> **Example**
>
> 03:00 is 3 o'clock in the morning. 15:00 is 3 o'clock in the afternoon.

3) The 12-hour clock goes from 12:00 am (midnight) to 11:59 am (one minute before noon), and then from 12:00 pm (noon) till 11:59 pm (one minute before midnight).

> **Example**
>
> 6 am is 6 o'clock in the morning. 6 pm is 6 o'clock in the evening.

4) For times in the afternoon, you need to add 12 hours to go from the 12-hour clock to the 24-hour clock. Take away 12 hours to go from the 24-hour clock to the 12-hour clock.

> **Example**
>
>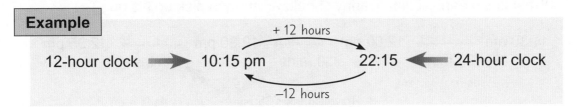

Working Out Lengths of Times

To work out how long something took, break it into stages.

> **Example**
>
> Ben set off on a walk at 12:45 and got back at 17:25.
> How long was his walk?
>
> 12:45 $\xrightarrow{\text{15 mins}}$ 13:00 $\xrightarrow{\text{4 hours}}$ 17:00 $\xrightarrow{\text{25 mins}}$ 17:25
>
> Add up the hours and minutes separately: 4 hours
> 15 mins + 25 mins = 40 mins
>
> So the walk took 4 hours and 40 mins.

Working Out Times

1) You may need to work out what time something will happen. For example, what time something will start or finish, when to meet someone or when something needs to start.

2) The best way to do this is to split the time into chunks.

Example 1

Ruth is going to watch a film at the cinema. The film lasts 2 hours and 30 minutes. There's a 15 minute interval in the middle of the film. If the film starts at 19:30, what time should the film end?

19:30 $\longrightarrow$ 21:30 $\longrightarrow$ 22:00 $\longrightarrow$ 22:15

2 hours   30 mins   15 mins

Film time   Interval

The film should finish at 22:45.

Example 2

Danny needs to pick his dog up from the vets.

He is getting his hair cut at 11:30 am which should take half an hour.

It will then take him about 35 minutes to travel to the vets.

What is the earliest time Danny should arrange to pick up his dog?

11:30 am $\longrightarrow$ 12:00 pm $\longrightarrow$ 12:30 pm $\longrightarrow$ 12:35 pm

30 mins   30 mins   5 mins

Length of hair cut

Travelling takes 35 mins — you can add it on in one go or break it down into 30 mins and 5 mins.

So the earliest he can be at the vets is 12:35 pm.
To be on the safe side he might arrange to be there at 12:45 pm.

Example 3

Jeremy and his friends are going out for the evening. They are going to a restaurant (a 15 minute journey), having a meal (taking about an hour and a half), before going to a play that starts at 8 pm (10 minutes' walk from the restaurant). What time do they need to set off?

8:00 pm $\longrightarrow$ 7:50 pm $\longrightarrow$ 6:20 pm $\longrightarrow$ 6:05 pm

-10 mins   -1 hour   -15 mins
          30 mins

The walk from   The meal takes   The journey to
the restaurant.   1 hour 30 mins.   the restaurant.

Working back from 8 pm this means they should set off by 6:05 pm.

Practice Questions

1) Change the times below from the 24-hour clock to the 12-hour clock.

   a)   08:30

   b)   19:57

   ....

   ....

2) Change the times below from the 12-hour clock to the 24-hour clock.

   a)   6:15 pm

   b)   12:03 am

   ....

   ....

3) Mischa has a bus to catch at 11:10 pm. The time is 22:59. Has she missed it?

   ....

4) A play starts at 8:30 pm and finishes at 11:00 pm. How long is the play?

   ....

   ....

5) Mike gets on a train at 10:55 am and gets off at 12:44 pm. How long was his train journey?

   ....

   ....

6) Cassandra arrives at the library at 4:28 pm. The library closes at 5:00 pm.
   How long does Cassandra have before the library closes?

   ....

   ....

7) Katie is doing her laundry. The washing machine cycle will take 70 minutes.
   If she put the washer on at 6:52 pm, what time will her washing be ready?

   ....

   ....

Section Two — Measure

Practice Questions

8) Charlotte wants to watch three half an hour episodes of a TV programme. She'll stop for 40 minutes to have dinner. If she starts watching at 16:45, what time will she finish?

....

....

....

9) Phillip plans to meet up with friends at 20:00.

He usually gets home from work at 6:00 pm.

Before he meets his friends he wants to go to the supermarket to do some shopping. He reckons he will need three quarters of an hour in the supermarket and it takes him 20 minutes to drive to the supermarket from his house.

When he gets back home it will take him 20 minutes to get to the meeting place.

Will he be able to meet his friends at 20:00?

....

....

....

....

10) Corinne is meeting her daughter for lunch in town at 1:15 pm. Before she meets her she needs to visit the florist and the bank. She thinks she'll be at the florists for about 25 minutes and at the bank for about 10. She wants to leave 20 mins for getting between the florist and the bank, and it will take her half an hour to walk to town.

What time should she leave home for town?

....

....

....

....

Timetables

Timetables Have Information About When Things Happen

1) Timetables have columns and rows.

2) Columns are the strips that go up and down. Rows are the strips that go across.

3) There are lots of different types of timetables — the best way to learn how to use them is to practise.

Example 1

The timetable below shows bus times.
What time would you need to leave Barrow to get to Ulverston for 15:30?

Barrow	14:10	14:30	14:50	15:10
Hospital	14:24	14:44	15:04	15:24
Dalton	14:36	14:54	15:16	15:36
Lindal	14:39	14:57	15:19	15:39
Swarthmoor	14:42	15:00	15:22	15:42
Ulverston	14:47	15:05	15:27	15:47

1) Find Ulverston in the timetable.

2) Follow that row until you reach the last time before 15:30. It's 15:27.

3) Go up the column till you reach the top row — the leaving time from Barrow.

4) So you'd need to leave Barrow at 14:50.

Example 2

Brendan works in a records office. His timetable for one week is below.

	Monday	Tuesday	Wednesday	Thursday	Friday
09:00-12:00	Archives	Help desk	Cataloguing	Help desk	Cataloguing
12:00-13:00	Lunch	Help desk	Lunch	Archives	Lunch
13:00-14:00	Help desk	Lunch	Archives	Lunch	Help desk
14:00-17:00	Cataloguing	Archives	Cataloguing	Cataloguing	Archives

1) What time is lunch on Wednesday? Answer: 12:00-13:00

2) Where will Brendan be at 1:30 pm on Monday? Answer: Help desk.

3) When will Brendan be in the archives on Tuesday? Answer: 14:00-17:00.

68

You Need to be Able to Create Timetables

There are no set rules for making timetables. You just need to use the information that you're given and fit it together the best way you can.

Example

Jack is a mechanic. He has four cars to work on today.
He has estimated how long he'll need to spend on each car:

> Mr Wills' car: 2½ hours   Mrs Fell's car: 1 hour
>
> Mr Nuttall's car: 1½ hours   Mr Goodwin's car: 1½ hours

Jack starts work at 08:00 and finishes at 16:00.

Work on Mr Wills' car and Mr Nuttall's car needs to be done before 14:00.
Work on Mrs Fell's car must be done first.

Jack gets an hour for lunch and a 10 minute break after every 2 hours of work.
Draw a timetable for his day.

Answer:

There are several different timetables that would work for this question.
Just make sure you follow all of the instructions from the question.

Here's an example of a timetable that would work:

The first job can start at 8:00.

Job	Time working From	To	Duration (minutes)
Mrs Fell's car	08:00	09:00	60
Mr Wills' car	09:00	10:00	60
Break	10:00	10:10	10
Mr Wills' car	10:10	11:40	90
Mr Nuttall's car	11:40	12:10	30
Break	12:10	12:20	10
Mr Nuttall's car	12:20	13:20	60
Lunch	13:20	14:20	60
Mr Goodwin's car	14:20	15:50	90

Make sure the correct amount of time is spent working on each car.

Make sure you put lunch at a sensible time.

The last job needs to have finished by 16:00 at the latest.

Section Two — Measure

Practice Questions

1) Look at the train timetable on the right.

York	14:13	15:08	16:00
Leeds	14:49	15:49	16:35
Hebden Bridge	15:37	16:38	17:10
Blackburn	16:14	17:14	17:38
Preston	16:32	17:32	18:03

   a) What's the latest train you can catch from York to get to Blackburn before 17:30?

   ....

   b) What time would you need to catch the train from Leeds to get to Preston before 6 pm?

   ....

2) Hazel is a mobile cleaner. Her bookings for the week are shown below. Hazel has been asked whether she can fit a two-hour slot for a new customer (Mrs Johnson) into her timetable. Suggest a time that Hazel could clean for Mrs Johnson.

	Mon	Tue	Wed	Thur	Fri
9:00	Mrs Simons		Day off		Mr Stevens
10:00	Mrs Simons	Mr Scarisbrick	Day off		Mr Stevens
11:00	Mrs Simons	Mr Scarisbrick	Day off	Mr Price	
12:00	Lunch	Mr Scarisbrick	Day off	Lunch	
13:00	Mrs Baldwin	Lunch	Day off	Dr Green	Lunch
14:00	Mrs Baldwin		Day off	Dr Green	Mr Sepp
15:00			Day off		Mr Sepp

   ....

3) A theatre is hosting a dance show that runs over two nights. The acts are shown in the table below. Each night the show starts at 7:30 pm and has two halves which are 90 minutes long. There is a 15 minute interval between them.

   In both shows, each half must contain three different styles of act.
   Each act's performance is 30 minutes long and can only be performed once a night.

   Plan a timetable for the shows.

Act	Style
Streetdance*	Urban
Camberwell	Urban
Super Eights	Swing
DUBDS	Belly
Xtreme Beats*	Urban
Salsa Stream	Salsa
Mirror Ball	Ballroom
Havanas	Latin

*Streetdance are only available on night 1.
 Xtreme Beats are only available on night 2.

2D and 3D Objects

Objects and Dimensions

1) Some objects are flat. Flat objects are called 2D objects.

2) Some objects are solid. Solid objects are called 3D objects.

3) The dimensions of an object tell you its size.

Examples

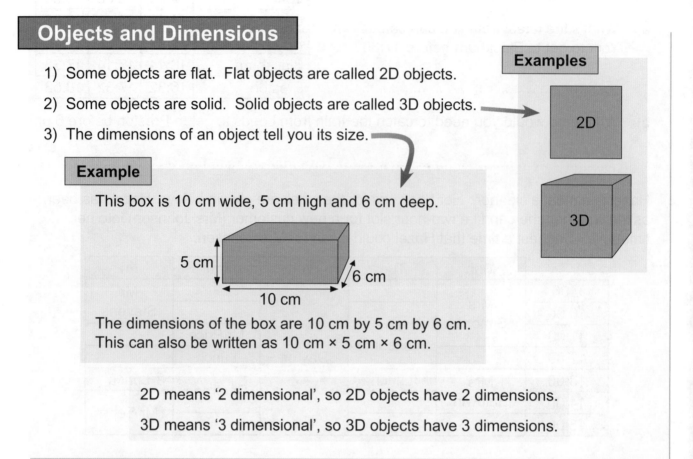

Example

This box is 10 cm wide, 5 cm high and 6 cm deep.

The dimensions of the box are 10 cm by 5 cm by 6 cm.
This can also be written as 10 cm × 5 cm × 6 cm.

2D means '2 dimensional', so 2D objects have 2 dimensions.

3D means '3 dimensional', so 3D objects have 3 dimensions.

You Need to be Able to Draw Nets

A net is just a 3D shape folded out flat. You can use a net to help you make a 3D object.

The nets for cubes and boxes always have the same basic shape.

Example 1

The cube has six sides, so the net of the cube has six squares.

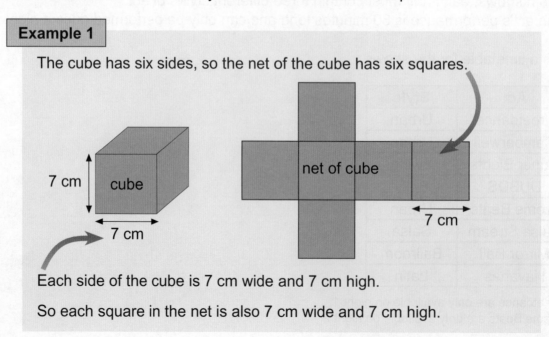

Each side of the cube is 7 cm wide and 7 cm high.

So each square in the net is also 7 cm wide and 7 cm high.

Example 2

Draw a net for the box below.

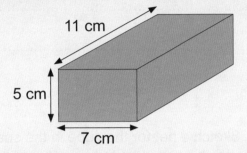

The box has 6 sides, so the net for the box will be made from 6 rectangles.

1) Draw the rectangle for the top of the box first.
   The diagram tells you it should be 11 cm long and 7 cm wide.

2) Next draw the rectangles for the sides of the box.
   The sides should be 11 cm long and 5 cm wide.

3) Now draw the rectangles for the front and back of the box.
   These should be 5 cm long and 7 cm wide.

4) Finally, draw the bottom of the box. The bottom of the box should be
   the same length and width as the top of the box.

You should end up with something like this:

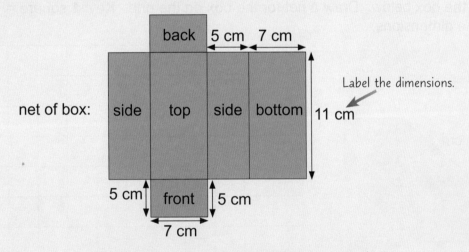

Tip: try to imagine your net being folded back up into the box.
If it works, there's a good chance you've got it right.

Practice Questions

1) Write down the dimensions of the box on the right.

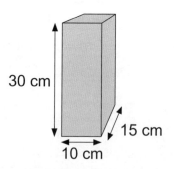

30 cm

10 cm

15 cm

....

....

2) A cube is shown below. Sketch a net for the cube in the space on the right.
Your sketch does not need to be accurate, but you should label the dimensions.

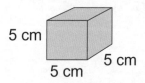

5 cm

5 cm

5 cm

3) Look at the box below. Draw a net for the box on the grid. Key: 1 square = 1 cm.
Label the dimensions.

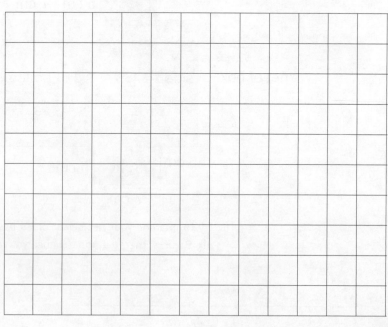

4 cm

2 cm

2 cm

2D Drawings of 3D Objects

You might be asked to draw accurate 2D drawings of 3D objects.
The 2D drawing you do depends on what angle you're looking at the object from.

Example

An architect is planning an extension
to a house, shown on the right.

Draw the side view of the house
on the grid provided.

1 square on the grid = 1 m in real life.

Start by drawing the dimensions you're given:

1) You know that the extension is 4 m wide.
   This is the same as 4 squares in your drawing.

2) You also know that the extension is 4 m high at
   the back and 3 m (3 squares) high at the front.

You can now draw the roof by connecting
the front and back walls. Your finished
drawing should look like this:

*Your drawing needs to be accurate, so make
sure you use a ruler and a sharp pencil.*

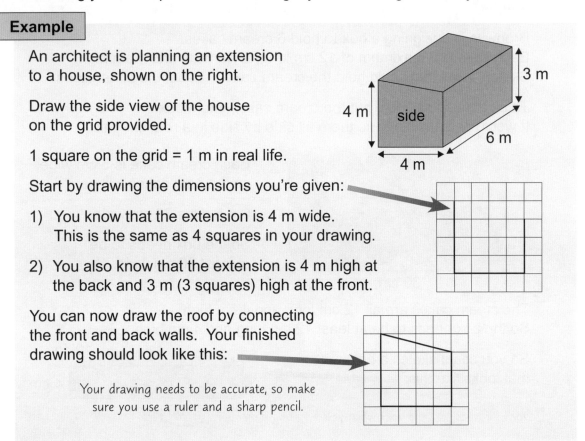

Practice Question

1) Gwyn is planning to make a doll's house for his daughter.
   A sketch of the doll's house is shown below on the right.

   On the grid below, draw an accurate side view of the doll's house.
   1 square on the grid = 10 cm in real life.

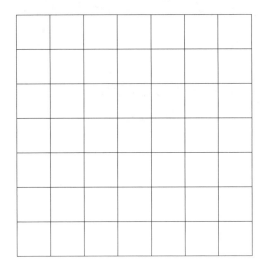

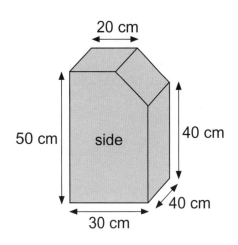

Working with Dimensions

You might get a question about 3D objects and their dimensions in your assessment.

Example

Bronwyn is designing a box to hold 6 cream cakes.
Each cake is a maximum of 12 cm long, 5 cm wide and 4 cm high.
Sketch a box that could hold the cream cakes. Label the dimensions.

Think about how you'd put the cream cakes into a box.
It would be sensible to lie them all side by side in a row, like this:

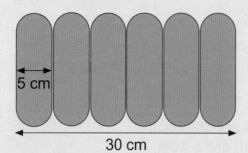

Each cream cake is 5 cm wide, so 6 cream cakes will be:

6 × 5 cm = 30 cm wide.

So the box needs to be at least 30 cm wide.

The cream cakes are all 12 cm long and 4 cm high.
So the box needs to be at least 12 cm long and 4 cm high.

So you could sketch a box that looks like this:

Don't forget to give the units when you're writing dimensions.

Practice Question

1) Stuart is posting some books to a friend. He wants a box to put them in.
The dimensions of the books are shown below.

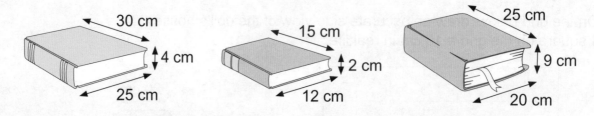

Sketch a box that could hold all the books. Label the dimensions of the box.

Symmetry

Some Shapes Have Lines of Symmetry

1) Shapes with a line of symmetry have two halves that are mirror images of each other.

2) You could fold a shape along this line and the sides would fold exactly together.

3) Some shapes have more than one line of symmetry.

Examples

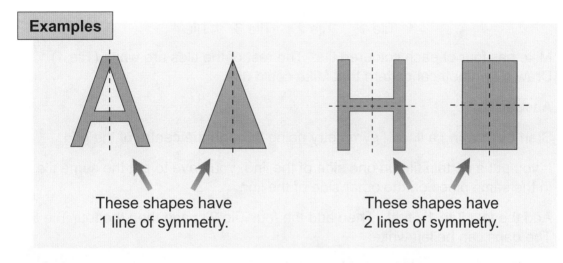

These shapes have
1 line of symmetry.

These shapes have
2 lines of symmetry.

4) Some shapes have no lines of symmetry.

Practice Questions

1) Draw the line (or lines) of symmetry on the shapes below:

a)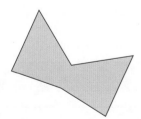

b)

c)

2) Complete the shapes below so they are symmetrical around the lines of symmetry.

a)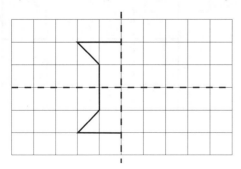

b)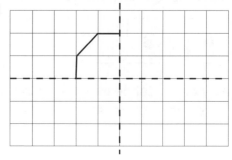

Symmetrical Patterns Have a Line of Symmetry

1) Patterns with a line of symmetry have two halves that are mirror images of each other.

2) You need to be able to draw symmetrical patterns.

Example

Mike is making a mosaic from coloured tiles. He wants to create a symmetrical design. The tiles Mike will use are shown below.

Tile 1   Tile 2   Tile 3   Tile 4

Mike has four of each coloured tile. The rest of the tiles are white (Tile 4). Draw a symmetrical pattern that Mike could use.

Answer:

Start by drawing a line of symmetry going through the centre of the grid.

If you put a certain tile on one side of the line, you have to put the same tile in the same place on the other side of the line.

Add the four Tile 1's first. Then add the four Tile 2's, and then the four Tile 3's. The gaps can be left white.

You might end up with something like this:

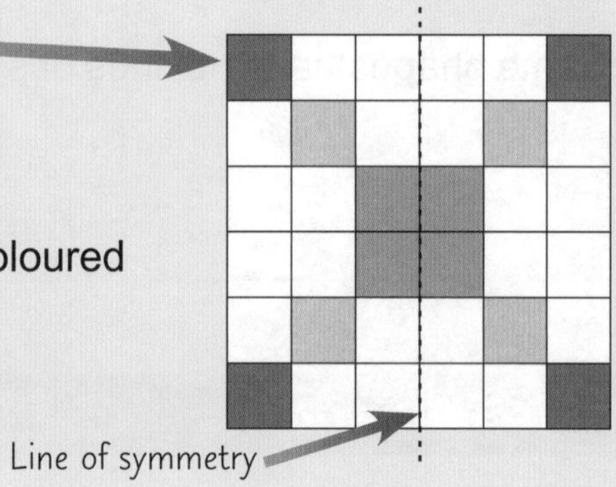

Double check that your pattern meets all the conditions in the question.

In this case, there needs to be four of each coloured tile and the pattern needs to be symmetrical.

There isn't just one right answer to this question. There are lots of different symmetrical patterns you could draw.

Line of symmetry

Practice Question

1) Kyla is tiling her bathroom wall. She wants a symmetrical design in the centre of the wall.

Kyla labels the tiles she wants to use as follows:

A   B   C   D

Draw a symmetrical design that Kyla could use in the grid on the right. You must use 4 of each type of tile.

Plans

Plans Show How Things are Laid Out in an Area

1) A plan shows the layout of an area. For example, a plan might show a room and all the objects in it.

2) Plans are drawn as if you are looking down on the area from above — a bird's eye view.

Example

A plan of an office is shown below:

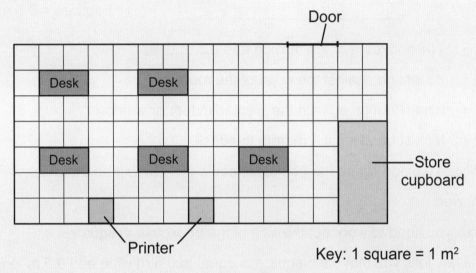

Key: 1 square = 1 m^2

On this plan each square on the grid represents 1 m^2 in the office.

This means that each square on the grid is equal to 1 m wide and 1 m long.

From this you can work out how large objects are and how far away things are from each other.

The store cupboard covers 8 squares.
This means the store cupboard has an area of: 8 × 1 m^2 = 8 m^2.

The room is 7 squares wide.
This means that the room is: 7 × 1 m = 7 m wide.

Using Plans

Plans are useful for deciding where a new object will fit in an area.

Example

Christine has bought a new bookcase for her study. She wants to know where to put the bookcase. A plan of the study is shown below.

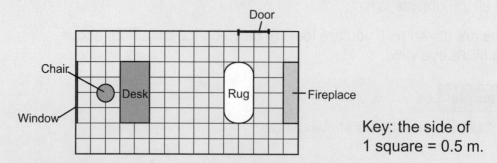

Key: the side of 1 square = 0.5 m.

- The bookcase is 1.5 m wide and 0.5 m deep.

- It must go against the edge of the room.

- It must not be against the fireplace, door or window.

- It must be at least 1 m from the desk.

Choose a place where the bookcase could go. Draw it on the plan.

Answer:

First, you need to work out the size of the bookcase in squares.

The key tells you that each square is equal to 0.5 m wide and 0.5 m long.

The bookcase is 0.5 m deep, so it must be 1 square deep.

The bookcase is 1.5 m wide: 1.5 ÷ 0.5 = 3.
So the bookcase is 3 squares wide.

The bookcase fits into the space along the bottom wall.

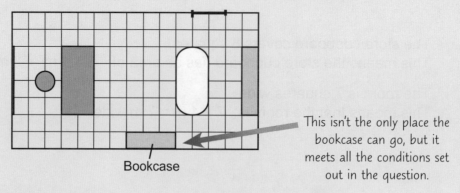

This isn't the only place the bookcase can go, but it meets all the conditions set out in the question.

Double check that the position of the bookcase meets all the conditions set out in the question.

For example, that it's at least 1 m (2 squares) from the desk.

Practice Questions

1) Dean has bought a plot of land. He wants to build two houses on it.
A plan of the land is shown below.

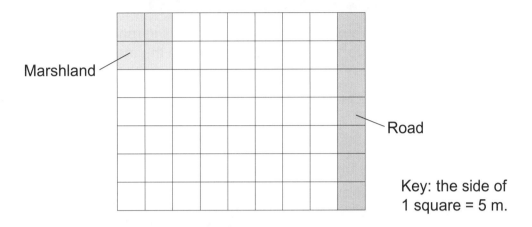

Each house should be 10 m wide and 15 m long.

The houses should be at least 5 m apart.

It is not possible to build on the marshland or the road.

Choose a place where each house could go. Draw them on the plan.

2) Lucy has bought a new table for her dining room. She wants to know
where to put it. A plan of Lucy's dining room is shown below.

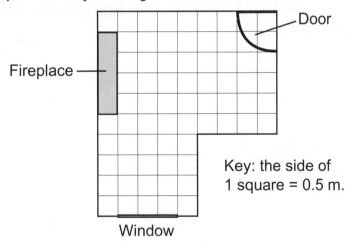

The table is 1.5 m wide and 2 m long.

Lucy wants to there to be a space of at least 0.5 m all the way around the edge of the table.

a) Draw on the plan where Lucy could put the table.

b) Lucy finds a cupboard that is 2.5 m wide and 1 metre deep. It must go against the edge
of the room, but shouldn't block the window, fireplace or door.

Is it possible to fit the cupboard in the room along with the dining table?

Maps and Map Scales

You Need to Know How to Use a Map Scale

1) A map scale tells you how far a given distance on a map is in real life.
   For example, a scale of 1 cm to 1 km means that 1 cm on the map equals
   1 km in real life.

2) You might be asked questions involving maps and map scales in your test.

Example 1

Look at the map. What is the distance between Fleetley and Coneston in km?

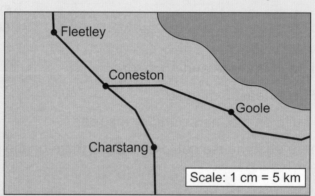

Scale: 1 cm = 5 km

1) Put your ruler against the bit you're finding the length of.
   Make sure the zero on the ruler is lined up with the starting place
   (in this case, Fleetley).

2) Mark off each whole cm and write
   the distance in km next to each one.
   In this case, 1 cm equals 5 km.

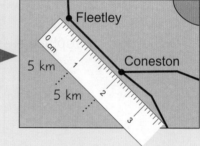

3) Add up all the km you just marked.
   So between Fleetley and Coneston:
   5 km + 5 km = 10 km.

Example 2

A map is drawn on a scale of 1 cm to 2 km.
If a road is 12 km long in real life, how long will it be in cm on the map?

Start by drawing the road as a straight line: ▢▢▢▢▢▢▢▢▢

Mark off each cm and fill in
how many km each one is:

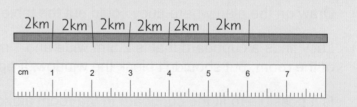

Keep going until the km add up to the full distance (12 km in this case).

Then just count how many cm long your line is — in this case it's 6 cm.

Practice Questions

1) A map is drawn with a scale of 1 cm to 4 km.

   a) If a road is 16 km in real life, how long will it be in cm on the map?

   ....

   ....

   b) If a road is 5 cm on the map, how long will it be in real life?

   ....

   ....

2) Simon is going to visit his friend Tim in Furly.
   He looks at a map to work out how far away Tim lives.

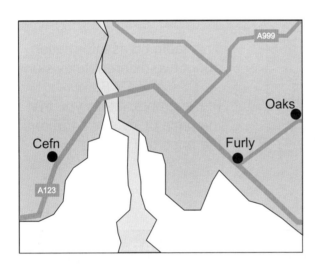

   Scale: 1 cm = 4 miles

   a) Simon lives in Oaks. How many miles will he have to travel to get to Tim's by road?

   ....

   ....

   b) Simon and Tim decide to drive from Tim's house to Cefn.
      How many miles is this journey?

   ....

   ....

   ....

   ....

Tables

Tables are a Way of Showing Data

Tables show information in columns and rows.

Examples

This table shows the names of staff based on different floors of an office block. ➡

This is a column.

Ground floor	First floor	Second floor
Tim	Mike	Janet
Jackie	Angela	Nick
Louis	Sarah	Brenda
Tony	Steve	Nicole
Steph	Drew	Anja

This is a row. ➡

This table has row headings as well as column headings.

	TV A	TV B
Screen	37 inch	40 inch
HD	720p	1080p
Colour	Black	Silver
Price (£)	450	550

This table holds information about two different televisions — TV A and TV B.
For example, it tells you that the price of TV A is £450 and the price of TV B is £550.

Mileage Charts give the Distances Between Places

Mileage charts tell you the distance between different places.

Example

Use the mileage chart on the right to find the distance from Bristol to Portsmouth.

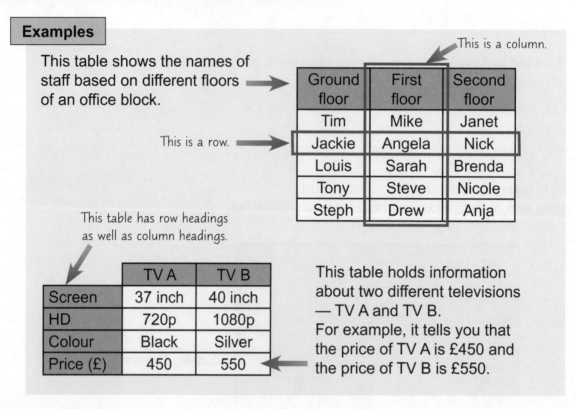

Exeter			
84	Bristol		
159	78	Reading	
128	93	54	Portsmouth

Distances are shown in miles.

1) Put fingers on 'Bristol' and 'Portsmouth' and move them towards each other.

2) Where your fingers meet is the distance between the two places — 93 miles.

Exeter			
84	Bristol		
159	78	Reading	
128	93	54	Portsmouth

Below is another type of mileage chart you might see.

Example

Use the mileage chart below to find the distance from Bristol to Portsmouth.

1) Find 'Bristol' on one side of the chart and 'Portsmouth' on the other.

2) Put fingers on 'Bristol' and 'Portsmouth' and move them towards each other — where your fingers meet is the distance between the two places.

3) It doesn't matter if you've followed the path of the green arrows or the black ones — the answer will be 93 miles.

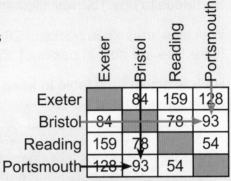

	Exeter	Bristol	Reading	Portsmouth
Exeter		84	159	128
Bristol	84		78	93
Reading	159	78		54
Portsmouth	128	93	54	

Distances are shown in miles.

Practice Questions

1) The table on the right shows details of three different hotels. Use the table to answer the following questions.

	Hotel A	Hotel B	Hotel C
Distance from city centre (miles)	0.5	1.2	0.1
Star rating	4	4	5
Parking?	Yes	Yes	No
Swimming pool?	Yes	No	Yes
Price per night (£)	86	72	112

a) How far is Hotel B from the city centre?

....

b) Which hotel is rated as 5-star?

....

c) Which hotel has parking and a swimming pool?

....

2) Use the mileage chart to answer the following questions. Distances shown are in miles.

York			
37.6	Bradford		
27.6	9.9	Leeds	
59.7	42.5	37.8	Sheffield

a) What is the distance between Bradford and Sheffield?

....

b) What is the distance between York and Leeds?

....

c) Steve is driving from York to Bradford and then on to Sheffield. How long is his journey?

....

Section Four — Handling Data

Completing Tables

You might be asked to complete a table as part of your test.

Example

Sam is re-tiling a bathroom in a house he is refurbishing.
He needs to buy 152 wall tiles and 29 floor tiles.

Wall tiles are sold in packs of 20 for £24.
Floor tiles are sold in packs of 15 for £22.50.

He has drawn up a table to keep track of his costs.
Complete the table below.

Type of tile	Number of tiles needed	Number of packs needed	Pack price (£)	Total cost (£)
Wall	152		24	
Floor	29		22.50	

1) Firstly, work out the number of packs needed.

   Number of packs needed = tiles needed ÷ number of tiles in a pack

   Wall tiles = 152 ÷ 20 = 7.60

   Floor tiles = 29 ÷ 15 = 1.93

   Sam can only buy whole packs of tiles, so he needs 8 packs of wall tiles and 2 packs of floor tiles — write this in the table.

Type of tile	Number of tiles needed	Number of packs needed	Pack price (£)	Total cost (£)
Wall	152	8	24	
Floor	29	2	22.50	

2) Next, work out the total cost for each type of tile.

   Total cost of each type of tile = number of packs needed x pack price

   Total cost of wall tiles = 8 × £24 = £192

   Total cost of floor tiles = 2 × £22.50 = £45

   Write your answers in the table.

Type of tile	Number of tiles needed	Number of packs needed	Pack price (£)	Total cost (£)
Wall	152	8	24	192
Floor	29	2	22.50	45

Practice Questions

1) Lynn is working out the number of days off that each of her employees should have next year. They all get 25 days off as standard, but some receive extra days.

Complete the table that Lynn has started below.

Employee	Standard days off	Extra days off	Total days off
Mike	25	5	
Sharon	25	2	
Lucy	25	0	
Phoebe	25	1	

2) Rikesh is supplying food for two weddings. He needs to work out how many food platters to supply to each party and the total cost of the platters. A platter serves 7 people and costs Rikesh £20 to make. Complete the table below.

	Number of guests	Number of platters required	Total cost of platters (£)
Wedding 1	120		
Wedding 2	80		

3) At a classic car show a group of cars are being judged to see which will win the 'best in show' award.

The judges give points to each car based on the interior, exterior and mechanical condition. For each of these criteria the judges can award up to 10 points.
The judges also look for modifications — cars lose 1 point for each modification they have.

Complete the table to show the final results.

	Interior score	Exterior score	Mechanical score	Number of modifications	Total score
Car 1	8	7	7	0	
Car 2	7	9	9	2	
Car 3	6	9	7	1	

Drawing Tables

Drawing Tally Charts and Frequency Tables

You can use a tally chart to put data into different categories.

Example

The tally chart below shows the types of fish caught by a fisherman.

Fish	Tally
Haddock	IIII
Cod	II
Plaice	II
Herring	Ⅲ II
Dab	I

There are 4 haddock.
There are 2 cod.
There are 2 plaice.
There are 7 herring.
There is 1 dab.

If another cod was caught by the fisherman you would add another line (tally mark) to the tally column next to cod.

In a tally, every 5th mark crosses a group of 4 like this: Ⅲ
So Ⅲ II represents 7 (a group of 5 plus 2).

You can add another column to make a frequency table.
You fill this in by adding up the tally marks for each fish.

Check the frequencies — the total should be the same as the number of tally marks (fish).

Colour	Tally	Frequency
Haddock	IIII	4
Cod	II	2
Plaice	II	2
Herring	Ⅲ II	7
Dab	I	1
		Total: 16

Practice Question

1) Julie's shop makes cakes for celebrations. Today she received orders for 2 birthday cakes, 2 wedding cakes, another birthday cake, a christening cake, a retirement cake, 3 Christmas cakes, another christening cake and another 2 birthday cakes.

a) Complete the table on the right using the information above.

b) How many birthday cake orders are there?

....

c) What was the total number of cake orders?

....

Type of cake	Tally	Frequency
Birthday		
Wedding		
Christening		
Retirement		
Christmas		
		Total

Designing Tables

1) Tables are useful for organising data so that it's easy to understand.

2) In the test you could be asked to design a table to collect or display data.

3) There isn't just one right way to do this — it all depends on what data the table needs to show.

4) If you're asked to draw a table make sure you...

- Include enough rows for all the data (if you know how much data will be stored in it) and any column or row headers that are needed.

- Include space to show everything the table needs to. (Check this again after you've drawn your table.)

- Think about how the table will be used — if you're using it to keep track of how many of something there are then a tally chart or a frequency table might be best.

Example

Laura is organising a dinner party for 8 guests. Some of her guests have special diets. The special diets are vegetarian, vegan, gluten-free and nut allergy.

Laura wants to design a table to show each guest's diet, as well as the total number of guests that have each type of diet. Some guests do not have a special diet — she wants to show this in the table as well.

The table could look like this:

| Guest | Special diet | | | | No special diet |
	Vegetarian	Vegan	Gluten-free	Nut allergy	
	Total:	Total:	Total:	Total:	Total:

There's space for each of the 8 guests' diets to be shown.

Make sure you include space for all the information — Laura wanted to include the total number of people with each diet so there needs to be somewhere to show that.

The type of diet for each guest can be shown by putting a tick under the diet type.

Practice Questions

1) Terry is an electrician. He needs to place an order with his supplier.

   Design a table that Terry could use to record the details of the order. The table should have space to record what items he is ordering, the number of each item he is ordering, the price of each item and the total cost of the order.

2) Debbie is organising a meal out for five family members.
   There are 3 choices of starter, 3 choices of main meal and 3 choices of dessert.

   Design a table that Debbie could use to record the choices of each guest and the total number of people ordering each option.

Bar Charts

Bar Charts Let You Compare Data Easily

1) A bar chart is a simple way of showing information.

2) On a bar chart you plot your data using two lines called axes
(if you're talking about just one then it's called an axis).

Example

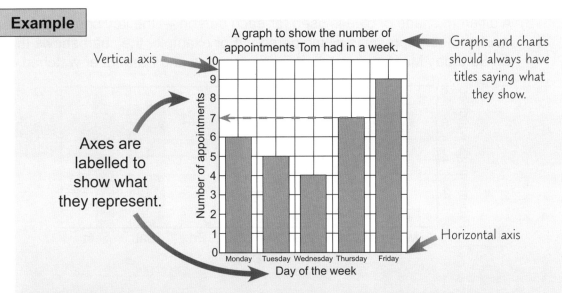

Vertical axis

Axes are labelled to show what they represent.

A graph to show the number of appointments Tom had in a week.

Graphs and charts should always have titles saying what they show.

Horizontal axis

1) The height of each bar shows how many appointments Tom had each day.

2) Just read across from the top of the bar to the number on the vertical axis.
For example, on Thursday Tom had 7 appointments.

3) You can draw conclusions from the chart. For example, you can see Tom
had the most appointments on Friday as it's the day with the tallest bar.

Practice Question

1) The bar chart shows the number of different colours of
kite that were seen at a kite festival.

a) How many green kites were seen?

....

b) Which colour was seen the most often?

....

c) How many kites were seen altogether?

....

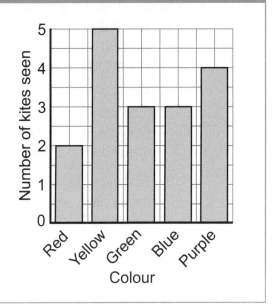

Dual Bar Charts Can be Used to Compare Data Sets

Dual bar charts show two sets of data at once so it's easy to compare the data. Each category has two bars — one for each data set.

Example

The dual bar chart below shows the number of TV programmes that Manpreet and Parminder watched in a week.

1) Each day has two bars — one for Manpreet and one for Parminder.

2) A different shade of blue is used for each person — the key shows you which colour represents which person. For example, the chart shows that on Saturday Manpreet watched 7 programmes and Parminder watched 4.

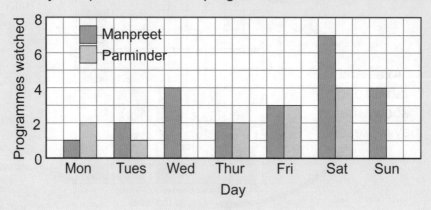

Composite Bar Charts Show Proportions

1) A composite bar chart has bars that are split into sections.

2) The height of the bar shows the total amount of something.

3) The sections show how that amount is broken down into different categories.

Example

1) The chart shows the number of men, women and children visiting a country show over 3 days.

2) The height of each bar shows the total number of visitors each day. For example, 200 people visited the show on Saturday.

3) The sections of the bars show how many men, women and children visited the show each day. For example, on Saturday 40 men, 70 women and 90 children visited the show.

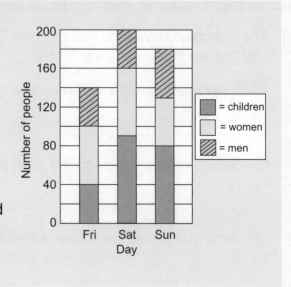

Practice Questions

1) A business sells clothes in a shop and also through its website.

The graph on the right shows the number of shop sales and online sales over the past 5 years.

a) How many shop sales were there in year 3?

....

b) How many more shop sales were there in year 2 than year 3?

....

c) How many more shop sales were there than online sales in year 3?

....

d) In which year were the number of shop sales and online sales the closest in number?

....

2) The bar chart below shows the destinations that a UK-based airline flew to over 3 years.

a) What percentage of flights were to Europe in year 1?

....

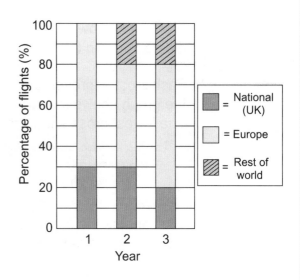

b) How much did the number of flights to Europe decrease by from year 1 to year 2?

....

c) In which year was the proportion of national flights and flights to the rest of the world the same?

....

d) Describe how the percentage of flights to places within the UK changed from year 1 to year 3.

....

....

Section Four — Handling Data

Line Graphs

Line Graphs Show the Relationship Between Two Things

Line graphs are similar to bar charts but instead of bars, a line is used to show the data.

Example

The line graph below shows how a motorhome's value changes over time.

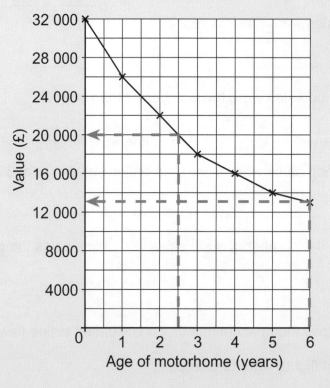

Sometimes line graphs don't have crosses on each plotted point — there's just a line to show the data.

1) The graph shows that the value of a motorhome goes down as it gets older. You can tell this because the line slopes downwards.

2) Each cross represents a data point. For example, the highest cross on the graph shows the motorhome was worth £32 000 when it was new. The lowest cross shows that a 6-year old motorhome is worth £13 000.

   The gap between each value on the vertical axis is 2 squares and represents £4000. This means each square represents £2000 and half a square represents £1000. So the point half a square above £12 000 represents a value of £13 000.

3) You can use the graph to find the value of a motorhome at any time up to 6 years. For example, to find the value after two and a half years...

   - Find the age on the horizontal axis — two and a half years is halfway between two years and three years.

   - Move directly upwards until you meet the line.

   - Go across from this point until you meet the vertical axis.
     The value at this point (£20 000) is the value after 2 and a half years.

Line Graphs Can Have More Than One Line On Them

If there's more than one set of data shown on a line graph you get more than one line.

Example

This graph shows rainfall in two different areas over 12 months.

There is a separate line to show rainfall in each region.

Using the graph it's easy to compare rainfall in the different regions. For example, in May, there was 60 mm of rainfall in Area B and 40 mm of rainfall in the Area A.

There's more on interpreting line graphs on page 101.

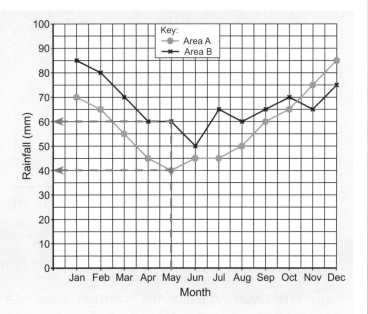

In Some Graphs the Points Aren't Joined Up

Some graphs just show the points — there's no line to join them up.

Example

The graph below shows the percentage of students at different colleges who passed an exam.

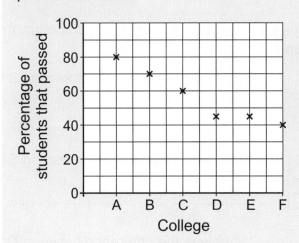

From the graph on the left you can read off the percentage of students who passed the test from each college.

For example, the college with the highest pass rate was college A (80% of students passed).
The college with the lowest pass rate was college F (only 40% of students passed).

Practice Questions

1) The graph below can be used for changing miles into kilometres.

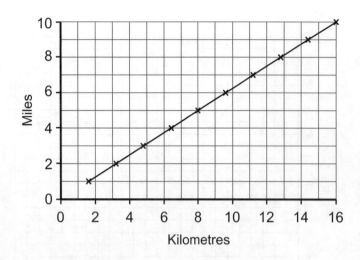

a) What is 5 miles in kilometres?

....

b) What is 12 kilometres in miles?

....

c) What is 14 kilometres to the nearest mile?

....

2) The line graph shows daily water use by two families — the Pearsons and the Cowells.

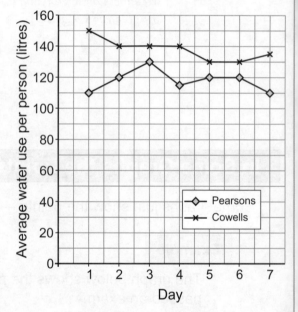

a) What was the Pearsons' average water use per person on day 3?

....

b) By how many litres did the Cowells' average water use per person fall from day 4 to day 5?

....

c) On which day was the difference between the two families' average water use per person the largest?

....

3) Dave has entered a cycling race for the past two years. He has drawn a line graph to compare his times for the different sections.

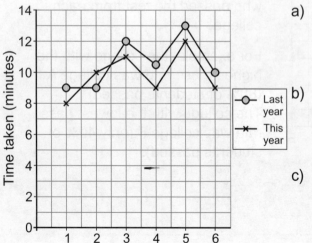

a) What was Dave's time for section 2 this year?

....

b) What was Dave's time for section 5 last year?

....

c) What was the difference between Dave's time for section 4 last year and this year?

....

Other Charts and Graphs

Pie Charts Show How Something is Split Up

1) Pie charts are circular and are divided into sections.

2) The size of each section depends on how much or how many of
something it represents.

Example

This pie chart shows the most popular activities at a leisure centre.

The size of each section shows how many people prefer that activity.

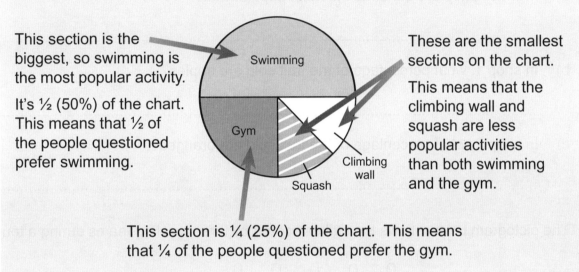

This section is the
biggest, so swimming is
the most popular activity.

It's ½ (50%) of the chart.
This means that ½ of
the people questioned
prefer swimming.

These are the smallest
sections on the chart.

This means that the
climbing wall and
squash are less
popular activities
than both swimming
and the gym.

This section is ¼ (25%) of the chart. This means
that ¼ of the people questioned prefer the gym.

Pictograms Use Pictures to Represent Numbers

1) Pictograms use pictures to show how many of something there are.

2) In a pictogram, each picture or symbol represents a certain number of items.

Example

The pictogram below shows the number of tickets sold at a cinema over 3 days.

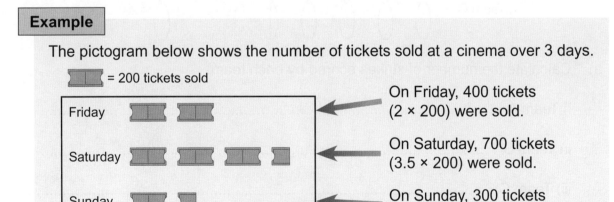

= 200 tickets sold

On Friday, 400 tickets
(2 × 200) were sold.

On Saturday, 700 tickets
(3.5 × 200) were sold.

On Sunday, 300 tickets
(1.5 × 200) were sold.

Total tickets sold = 400 + 700 + 300 = 1400 tickets.

Practice Questions

1) A sales manager is looking at the sales of fruit in two different shops.

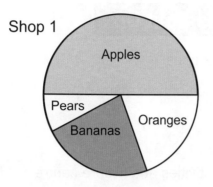
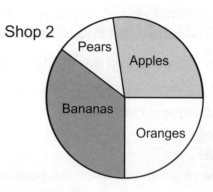

   a) In which shop are bananas the most popular fruit?

   ....

   b) In shop 1, what percentage of the fruit sold are apples?

   ....

   c) In shop 2, what percentage of the fruit sold are oranges?

   ....

2) The pictogram below shows the strikes scored by three bowling teams during a tournament.

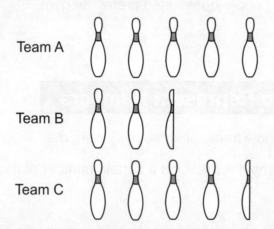

= 10 strikes

   a) Calculate the number of strikes scored by each team.

   i) Team A ....

   ii) Team B ....

   iii) Team C ....

   b) In total, how many strikes were scored by the three teams?

   ....

Drawing Charts and Graphs

Drawing Bar Charts

You need to know how to draw a bar chart. The main steps are choosing what the axes will represent, choosing a scale for the axes and plotting (drawing) the data.

Example

The table below shows the monthly sales of a newspaper over 6 months. Draw a bar chart to show this data.

1) The bar chart will need to show the months and the number of newspapers (in thousands) that were sold. So these are what the axes will represent.

Month	Newspaper sales (thousands)
January	25
February	23
March	24
April	20
May	22
June	26

2) Work out a scale for the axes. (This is how the units will be spaced out along each axis.)

The biggest number of newspapers sold in a month is 26 000. So the axis needs to go from 0 to at least 26 000.

By giving the units as thousands you can just write, e.g. 26 on the scale.

Make sure the axes are clearly labelled.

1 square = 2000 newspapers.

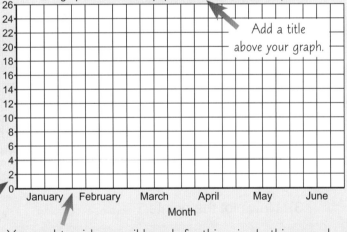

Add a title above your graph.

You need to pick a sensible scale for this axis. In this example, each bar will be 2 squares wide, with a 2 square gap between each bar.

3) Use a ruler to draw on the bars.

Make sure the bars are all the same width, and that the gaps between the bars are equal.

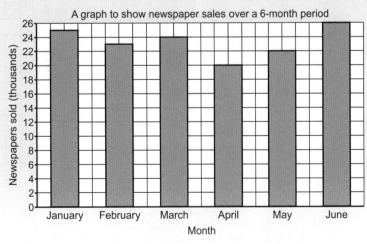

Drawing Line Graphs

The main steps for drawing line graphs are choosing what the axes will represent, choosing a scale for the axes and plotting the points.

Example

The growth of a tree over a period of 10 years is shown in the table. Show this data on a line graph.

1) The line graph will need to show the year and the trunk diameter.

   So the diameter of the trunk and the year are what the two axes will represent.

Year	0	2	4	6	8	10
Trunk diameter (inches)	3	5	7	8.5	10.5	12

2) Work out the scales for the axes.

Trunk diameter needs to go up to at least 12 inches — the highest diameter recorded.

Add labels to your axes. Make sure you include the units (inches).

If you use 1 square to represent 1 inch you need at least 12 squares for this axis.

Year needs to go from 0 to 10. Each square represents a year.

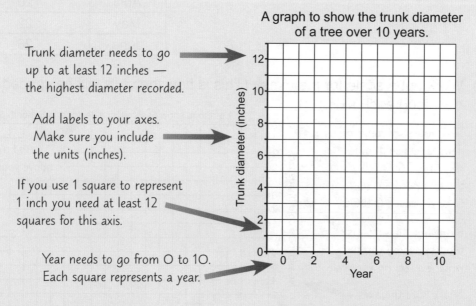

A graph to show the trunk diameter of a tree over 10 years.

3) Now plot the points.

For example, by year 4 the trunk diameter was 7 inches. Put one finger on the year (4) and move it up until you reach the diameter of the trunk (7) — draw a cross here.

Once you've plotted the points, join them with straight lines.

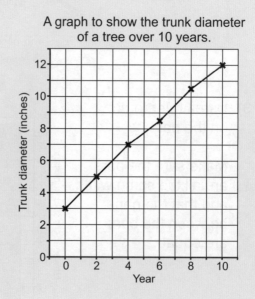

A graph to show the trunk diameter of a tree over 10 years.

Plotting Two Sets of Data

1) You may have to draw a chart or graph that shows more than one set of data. For example, a dual or composite bar chart or a line graph with more than one line.

2) You have to do all the same things that you would do when drawing a chart or graph for a single set of data, but there are a few extra things to think about too...

Plotting Two Sets of Data on a Bar Chart

When you're drawing a bar chart with more than one set of data you need to remember to do these things...

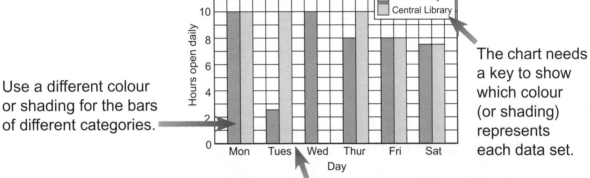

Use a different colour or shading for the bars of different categories.

The chart needs a key to show which colour (or shading) represents each data set.

Leave enough space on your horizontal axis for two bars at each data point if you're drawing a dual bar chart.

Plotting Two Sets of Data on a Line Graph

When you're drawing a line graph with more than one set of data you need to remember to do these things...

Make each line clearly different. You can do this by using a different colour for each line...

...and by using different symbols (for example crosses and dots) for plotting the points of different data sets.

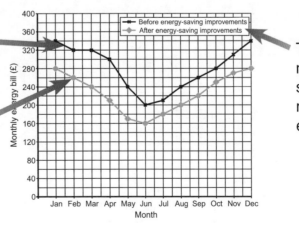

The graph needs a key to show which line represents each data set.

Practice Questions

1) A company sells cars in different regions of the UK. The number of petrol and diesel cars it has sold over the past 6 months are shown in the unfinished dual bar chart below.

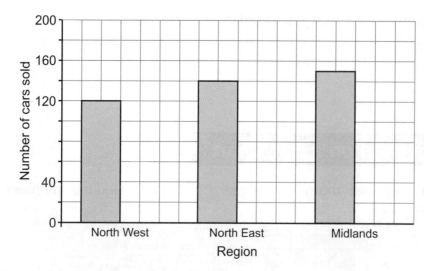

	Diesel
North West	150
North East	
Midlands	180

a) How many petrol cars were sold in the North West?

....

b) The sales of diesel cars in the North West and Midlands are shown in the table. Add these as bars to the chart.

c) In the North East 20 more diesel cars than petrol cars were sold. Add a bar to show the sales of diesel cars.

d) There is a number label missing from the vertical axis. Add this to the chart.

2) The amount of water left in the hot water tank of a house over the course of a day is shown in the table below. Draw a line graph to show how the amount of water changes.

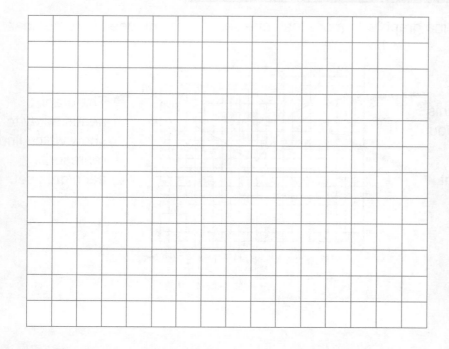

Time	Hot water remaining (litres)
06:00	90
09:00	40
12:00	35
15:00	35
18:00	10

Interpreting Data

You Need to Be Able to Interpret Graphs

1) You can get a lot of information from looking at a graph.

2) As well as reading off specific measurements, you can look at the data as a whole and spot any trends (patterns). You can also compare different data sets.

Example

The graph below shows sales of footwear and clothing from a group of outdoor shops.

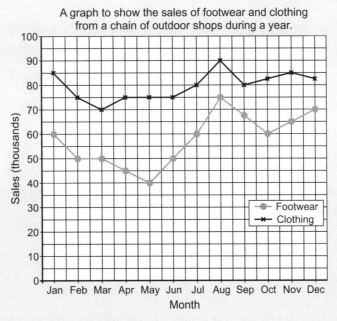

A graph to show the sales of footwear and clothing from a chain of outdoor shops during a year.

From the graph you can see that:

1) Clothing sales are higher than footwear sales in every month of the year — the black line (clothing) is always higher than the blue line (footwear).

2) The sales of both clothing and footwear are highest in August — you can see this as the highest point on each line is in August.

3) There are differences in the sales of clothing and footwear during the year too. For example...

Footwear sales increase each month from October to December — the line slopes upwards from October to December.

But clothing sales don't change much during this time — the line slopes upwards slightly in November but goes back down to the same level as October in December.

You Also Need to Be Able To Interpret Tables and Other Data

In the test you might have to look at some data and say what it shows.

Example 1

Carl is a railway station manager. One of the trains that comes through the station is often delayed. The average lengths of the delay are shown below.

	Jun	Jul	Aug	Sept	Oct	Nov	Dec
Average length of delay (minutes)	8	7.7	7.8	7	7	6.8	6.5

Carl says that the average length of the delay has been reduced by 20% in 6 months. Is he right?

1) In June, the average delay was 8 minutes. Six months later the average delay was 6.5 minutes. So the delay has been reduced by...

$$8 - 6.5 = 1.5 \text{ mins}$$

2) Work out what percentage of 8 minutes 1.5 minutes is...

$$\frac{1.5}{8} \times 100 = 18.75\%$$

3) So Carl is wrong — the average length of the delay has been reduced by 18.75%, not 20%.

Example 2

The table below shows the sales of hot and cold drinks from a drinks stand at a range of average outdoor temperatures.

Average temperature (°C)	16.2	18.1	19.7	19.9	22	24.7
Number of hot drinks sold	21	20	19	17	13	12
Number of cold drinks sold	4	7	12	23	41	68

What can you say about the relationship between the average temperature and the number of hot and cold drinks sold?

Answer:

The number of cold drinks sold increases as the average temperature increases. The number of hot drinks sold decreases as the average temperature increases.

Practice Questions

1) A company has two call centres. The target time for answering a phone call is 45 seconds. The bar chart shows the percentage of calls answered in the target time at each call centre.

Which of the call centres was more successful at answering calls in the target time?
Explain your answer.

....

....

....

....

A chart to show the percentage of calls answered in the target time at two call centres

2)

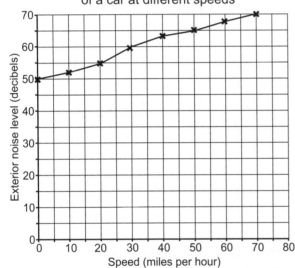

A graph to show the exterior noise level of a car at different speeds

The graph on the left shows the exterior noise level of a car at different speeds.

Describe what the graph shows about exterior noise levels and speed.

....

....

....

....

3) The table below shows the number of hours 5 people work per week and their annual income.

	Helen	Joseph	Martha	Leo	Eugenia
Number of hours worked per week	37.5	32	36	10	26
Annual income (£)	27 500	17 500	13 500	8600	16 400

Write two statements to describe the information shown in the table

....

....

....

Averages

The Mean is a Type of Average

1) An average is a number that summarises a lot of data. For example, the average national salary is worked out from the salaries of everyone in the country.

2) The mean is one of several different types of average.

> To work out the mean:
>
> 1) Add up all the numbers.
>
> 2) Divide the total by how many numbers there are.

Example 1

The table shows the broadband speeds of a group of residents in a town. What is the mean broadband speed?

1) First, add up the numbers:
   6.7 + 13.6 + 7.9 + 12.2 + 17.1 = 57.5

2) There are 5 numbers so divide the total by 5:
   57.5 ÷ 5 = 11.5

3) The mean is 11.5 Mb.

Resident	Speed (Mb per second)
Mr Stewart	6.7
Mrs Fisher	13.6
Mr Ward	7.9
Mrs Ford	12.2
Mrs Wells	17.1

Example 2

Martyn is moving house. He is trying to decide which of 3 houses he should buy. For work he travels between three different offices and would like to live in the house which has the lowest mean distance to all three of them.
Use the information in the table to decide which house he should choose.

	Distance from office sites (miles)		
	House 1	House 2	House 3
North office	27	33	36
East office	33	6	21
West office	12	39	12

Work out the total distance each house is from all the offices then divide this by the number of offices (3).

House 1:   27 + 33 + 12 = 72   72 ÷ 3 = 24 miles
House 2:   33 + 6 + 39 = 78   78 ÷ 3 = 26 miles
House 3:   36 + 21 + 12 = 69   69 ÷ 3 = 23 miles

House 3 has the lowest mean distance from all the offices (23 miles), so Martyn should choose house 3.

Sometimes you already have the total and just need to divide it to get the mean.

Example 3

The total weight of 15 containers on a freight train is 330 tonnes.
On average, how much does each container weigh?

1) To find the mean weight of each container you need to divide the total weight by the number of containers.
   330 tonnes ÷ 15 tonnes = 22 tonnes

2) The mean weight of a container is 22 tonnes. *This doesn't mean that every container weighs 22 tonnes. Some might do, but others might weigh more or less — it's just an average.*

Estimating Using Means

1) You may be asked to estimate a total amount from a given mean.

2) To do this, multiply the mean by the number of items (for example) that you are given in the question.

Example

Sheila makes wool jumpers. The jumpers take a mean time of 30 hours each to make. How long will it take her to make 5 jumpers?

To work out the total time you need to multiply the mean time by the number of jumpers.

30 hours × 5 = 150 hours

The Median is Another Type of Average

The median is the middle value of a set of data when the values are arranged in size order.

Example

For the following data work out the median.

10, 6, 4, 7, 9, 2, 9, 3, 3, 7 and 9.

1) Firstly, arrange the data in order of size: 2, 3, 3, 4, 6, 7, 7, 9, 9, 9, 10

2) The median is the middle value, 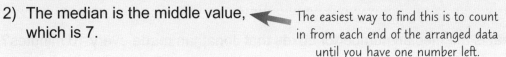 *The easiest way to find this is to count in from each end of the arranged data until you have one number left.*
   which is 7.

The Mode is Also a Type of Average

The mode is the most common value that appears in a set of data.

Example

For the following data work out the mode.

10, 6, 4, 7, 9, 2, 9, 3, 3, 7 and 9.

1) Firstly, arrange the data in order of size: 2, 3, 3, 4, 6, 7, 7, 9, 9, 9, 10

2) The mode is 9 as it appears more than any other number (three times).

Practice Questions

1) A small business records the amount of money customers spend on its website. The totals for the last 10 days are: £6750, £1225, £5643, £3633, £2600, £1512, £4570, £5080, £2287 and £4671. What is the mean amount spent online?

....

....

2) A group of 9 cars have a total weight of 16 920 kg. What is the mean weight of the cars?

....

....

3) Siobhan has been timing her journey to work for the past 7 days.
The times she recorded are: 45 mins, 36 mins, 29 mins, 40 mins, 32 mins, 38 mins, 44 mins.
What is Siobhan's median journey time?

....

....

4) At a factory Jonathan makes boxes. The number of boxes he can make in 10 minute periods has been counted. The numbers he made were: 8, 7, 8, 7, 6, 8, 6.

a) What is the mode number of boxes that Jonathan made every 10 minutes?

....

b) What is the median number of boxes that Jonathan made every 10 minutes?

....

Range

The Range is the Gap Between Biggest and Smallest

The range is the difference between the biggest value and the smallest value.

To work out the range:

1) Write down all the numbers in order from the smallest to the biggest.

2) Subtract the smallest number from the biggest number.

Example

Babies are weighed when they are born. The weights of the babies born at a hospital this week in kilograms are: 2.2, 3.6, 2.6, 4.1, 4.0, 2.9, 2.4 and 3.2. Work out the range in the weight of newborn babies.

1) First, write the weights in order of size:
2.2, 2.4, 2.6, 2.9, 3.2, 3.6, 4.0, 4.1.

2) Subtract the smallest number (2.2) from the biggest (4.1).

Range = 4.1 − 2.2 = 1.9 kilograms.

Practice Questions

1) Work out the ranges of the following sets of data.

a) 3, 2, 6, 7, 11, 15, 8, 10.

....

b) 23.4, 36.5, 67.2, 22.2, 52.2, 43.7.

....

2) Jeremy goes for a run every day after work for two weeks. He records the distance he covered each day in miles. They are: 2.2, 3.6, 2.9, 4.8, 4.6, 2.7, 5.2, 5.5, 4.3 and 3.7.

a) What is the range of the distances that Jeremy ran?

....

....

b) Jeremy recorded the last distance incorrectly. It should have been 4.7 miles rather than 3.7 miles. Would using the correct distance change the range?

....

Using Averages and Range

Averages and Ranges can be Applied to Many Examples

You can use averages and ranges in real life examples.

Example 1

The table below shows the practice lap times set by three racing drivers. Which driver has been setting the most consistent times?

Driver	Lap Times (seconds)				
	Lap 1	Lap 2	Lap 3	Lap 4	Lap 5
Smithson	54	52	53	55	51
Olivier	49	56	55	57	53
Durango	51	54	56	55	52

1) To answer this you can use the range of times the driver has set.

   A small range of lap times for a driver means their times are all quite similar, so they are consistent. A large range means that the driver's times are not very consistent.

   Smithson's range = 55 secs – 51 secs = 4 seconds
   Olivier's range = 57 secs – 49 secs = 8 seconds
   Durango's range = 56 secs – 51 secs = 5 seconds

2) So the most consistent driver is Smithson, who had the smallest range of times (4 seconds) across his practice laps.

Example 2

Joe and Annette want to book a hotel. They have found some reviews online for two hotels (shown below). Each category has been scored out of 5.

		Review 1	Review 2	Review 3	Review 4	Review 5
Well	Location	4	4	3	3	3
Bridge	Service	4	3	3	3	4
Hotel	Rooms	4	3	2	3	3

		Review 1	Review 2	Review 3	Review 4	Review 5
Old	Location	5	4	5	4	4
Mill	Service	4	5	4	3	5
Hotel	Rooms	3	2	4	3	3

Which hotel has better reviews?

There is more than one way of answering this question but you need to use the information in the table to support any answers you give.

For example, you could work out the mean score for location, service and rooms for each hotel and then compare them.

	Mean Score		
	Location	Service	Rooms
Well Bridge Hotel	3.4	3.4	3
Old Mill Hotel	4.4	4.2	3

From these means, the Old Mill Hotel looks like it has better reviews.

Practice Question

1) Jen wants to go on holiday with her husband.
The table below shows prices from 4 different travel companies.

	Fly Well	City Hols	Destination City	City Escapes
3 days	£580	£597	£479	£560
4 days	£635	£675	–	£730

a) What is the range and mean cost of a 3-day package from the 4 companies?

....

....

b) Destination City don't offer 4-day packages.
What is the range and mean cost of a 4-day package from the other 3 companies?

....

....

c) Jen thinks that Fly Well offers cheaper holidays than City Escapes. Is she right?

....

....

....

Probability

Probability is all About Likelihood and Chance

1) Likelihood is how likely an event is to happen.

2) There are some key words you need to know:

- Certain — this is when something will definitely happen.
  For example, getting a number between 1 and 6 when you roll a dice.

- Likely — this is when something isn't certain, but there's a high chance it will happen. For example, it's likely that it will rain during the summer in the UK.

- Even chance — this is when something is as likely to happen as it is not to happen. For example, there's an even chance of getting heads when you toss a coin.

- Unlikely — this is when something isn't impossible, but it probably won't happen. For example, it's unlikely you'll win the jackpot in the lottery.

- Impossible — this is when there's no chance at all of something happening. For example, it's impossible to roll a 7 on a standard six-sided dice.

3) An event being impossible isn't the same as one that is very very unlikely. For example, it's very very unlikely that it won't rain in the UK in winter, but it's not impossible.

Numbers can be Used to Describe Probability

Fractions, decimals and percentages can all be used to describe probability.

- If something is impossible, it has a probability of 0 (or 0%).

- If something has an even chance of happening, it has a probability of 0.5 (or ½ or 50%).

- If something is certain, it has a probability of 1.0 (or 100%).

- If something is likely, the probability of it happening is between 0.5 and 1.
  The more likely it is, the closer it will be to 1.

- If something is unlikely, the probability of it happening is between 0.5 and 0.
  The less likely it is, the closer it will be to 0.

Probability can be Shown on a Scale

The probability of something can be shown on a scale between 0 and 1 — see below.

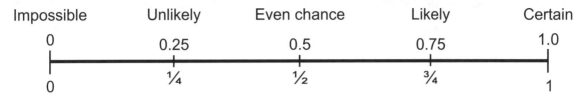

Impossible   Unlikely   Even chance   Likely   Certain

0   0.25   0.5   0.75   1.0

0   ¼   ½   ¾   1

Example

What is the probability of getting a head when tossing a coin?

There is an even chance of getting a head or a tail so the probability is ½ (or 0.5 or 50%). This can be shown on a probability scale:

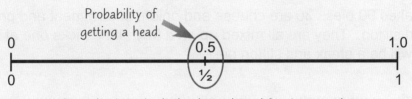

Probability of getting a head.

0   0.5   1.0

0   ½   1

In the scale above both the decimals and fractions are shown, but in the test you would only need to show one of them.

You May Need to Calculate a Probability

Sometimes you'll need to work out the probability of something happening.

Example 1

Sam is a hockey club coach. He divides the team of 16 players by asking each player to draw a ticket at random from a hat. The hat contains 4 blue, 4 green, 4 red and 4 yellow tickets. What is the probability of the first player to pick getting a blue ticket?

There are 16 tickets in total and 4 blue tickets so the probability is $\frac{4}{16}$ or more simply $\frac{1}{4}$

You can also give the probability as a percentage (25%) or a decimal (0.25).

Example 2

Mohini has brought a box of apples into work to share with her colleagues. There are 5 green apples and 9 red apples.
What is the probability of picking a red apple out of the box at random?

There are 14 apples in total and 9 red apples so the probability is $\frac{9}{14}$ ← *You need to give this probability as a fraction because it doesn't give an exact decimal.*

Practice Questions

1) James thinks it's impossible to have warm and sunny weather in the UK during December. Is he right? Explain your answer.

....

....

2) Sophia has a pack of buttons containing 4 blue, 6 pink, 8 white and 6 red buttons. She picks one out without looking. What is the probability of Sophia picking a red button?

....

3) Simon has baked 90 pies. 30 are cheese and onion, 30 are meat and potato and the others are steak and stilton. They are all mixed up on a tray. If he picks one at random what is the probability it will be a steak and stilton pie?

....

4) A travel company has a fleet of 16 coaches. 12 are painted black and 4 are painted white. At the start of the day all the coaches are available and Geoff picks up a set of coach keys.

   a) What is the probability he has the keys to a white coach?
      Give the probability as a fraction, a decimal and a percentage.

   ....

   ....

   b) What is the probability he has the keys to a black coach?
      Give the probability as a fraction, a decimal and a percentage.

   ....

   ....

5) Rachel has made ten necklaces to sell at a craft fair. 8 of them have a quartz set into them and the other two have moonstones instead.

   a) Whilst unpacking them, what is the chance that Rachel picks a quartz necklace out first? Give the probability as a fraction, a decimal and a percentage.

   ....

   b) Show the probability of picking out a quartz necklace on a probability scale.
      Label the scale with the probability in decimals.

Test Help

Always Show Your Working

1) In the test it's really important that you show all of your working — there are lots of marks for the methods you use and the calculations that you do.

2) If you don't show how you worked your answer out, you may not get all of the marks — even if your final answer is right.

3) So, even if you type a calculation into your calculator to work it out, you must write the calculation down for the examiner to see as well.

You May Have to Use an Answer in Another Calculation

1) Sometimes you may need to use the answer to one question to work out the answer to another question.

2) If you get the answer to the first question wrong, you'll also get the answer to the second one wrong.

3) BUT if you use the right method, and you use the answer that you got for the first question in your calculation, then you can still get full marks for the second question.

4) So even if you're unsure about an answer, don't give up — make sure you keep going until the end of the question.

Always Check Your Answers

It's really important that you check your answers. Checking your answers helps you to spot mistakes that you've made, and in some questions there are marks for showing that you've checked your answer. There are lots of ways you can check answers. For example...

1) Reverse the calculation (see pages 2 and 3 for more on this).

2) Do the calculation again using a different method to see if you get the same answer.

3) Think about whether your answer is sensible. For example, if you're working out the cost of someone's lunch and your answer comes out as hundreds of pounds then you've probably made a mistake somewhere.

Task 1 — Banking and Finance

1. Sean earns £23 500 per year, and has £10 000 saved up for a deposit on a new flat

    Sean has seen a flat for sale for £55 000.

    He has received a letter from his bank about taking out a mortgage.

PGS Bank

Dear Mr Bourne

I can confirm that we can lend you up to 3 times your salary as a mortgage.

You will need to pay at least one fifth of the value of the property as a deposit.

Please make an appointment to see one of our advisors to discuss this further.

Yours sincerely

Dan Le Maison

PGS Mortgages

---

a)   Can he buy the flat under the conditions given by PGS in the letter above?

....

....

....

....

....

....

(3 marks)

b) Sean decides to talk to another bank about their mortgage deals.

We can lend you up to 2½ times your salary. You'll need to pay 15% of the value of the property as a deposit.

Can he buy the flat with a mortgage from this new bank?

....

....

....

....

....

....

....

(3 marks)

2.   Danni is starting a new job as an outdoors instructor. She will be paid £16 000 a year. She wants to work out how much tax she will have to pay.

Working out your Income Tax — *A Helpful Guide*

<u>If you earn up to £35 000:</u>
You will not be taxed on the first £7475.
You will be taxed 20% on the rest of your money.

<u>If you earn between £35 001 and £150 000:</u>
You will not be taxed on the first £7475.
You will be taxed 20% on any amount between £7476 and £35 000.
You will be taxed 40% on the rest of your money.

<u>If you earn over £150 000:</u>
You will not be taxed on the first £7475.
You will be taxed 20% on any amount between £7476 and £35 000.
You will be taxed 40% on any amount between £35 001 to £150 000.
You will be taxed 50% on the rest of your money.

---

a)   Using the guide above, how much income tax will Danni have to pay each year?

....

....

....

....

....

....

(2 marks)

b)   Just before Danni starts work, the rules for paying income tax change.
     A new guide to working out your income tax is published.

NEW:Working out your Income Tax — *A Helpful Guide*

If you earn up to £34 370:
You will not be taxed on the first £8105.
You will be taxed 20% on the rest of your money.

If you earn between £34 371 and £150 000:
You will not be taxed on the first £8105.
You will be taxed 20% on any amount between £8106 and £34 371.
You will be taxed 40% on the rest of your money.

If you earn over £150 000:
You will not be taxed on the first £8105.
You will be taxed 20% on any amount between £8106 and £34 371.
You will be taxed 40% on any amount between £34 371 to £150 000.
You will be taxed 50% on the rest of your money.

Under these new rules, how much less income tax will Danni have to pay each year?

....

....

....

....

....

....
                                                                                        (3 marks)

118

3.   Emily takes out a loan to buy a car for £6750.

She wants to pay it back in full, including the interest, in 12 equal monthly instalments.

Annual interest rates for loans

Amount Borrowed	Interest Rate
less than £5000	17%
£5000 - £10 000	15%
more than £10 000	13%

Repayment calculations:
Monthly repayments are calculated by adding the interest amount to the amount borrowed and splitting the total into equal monthly repayments.

How much will Emily have to pay each month, to the nearest penny?

....

....

....

....

....

....
                                                                                (3 marks)

Task 2 — Landscape Gardening

4.   Harry is building a pond in his garden.
     He wants to put a border made of tiles around the pond.

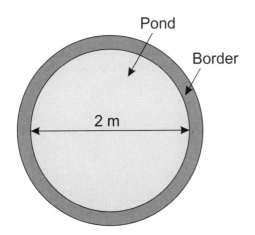

Pond

Border

2 m

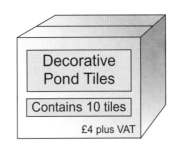

Decorative
Pond Tiles

Contains 10 tiles

£4 plus VAT

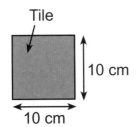

Tile

10 cm

10 cm

Perimeter of a circle (in m) = π × diameter (in m)

You may use π = 3.14.   VAT = 20%

a)   How many boxes of tiles will Harry need to buy to go all the way around the pond?

....

....

....

....

....

....

....

(5 marks)

b)   How much will the tiles cost Harry in total?

....

....

....

....

(2 marks)

5.   Jordan is redesigning his garden. He wants to have a lawn and one large flower bed.
      He will need to order turf for his lawn. A plan of Jordan's garden is shown below.

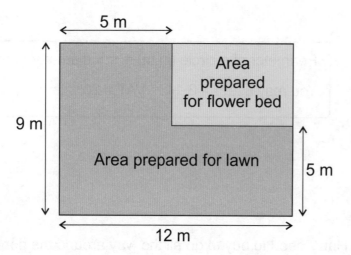

Turf Shack

We sell turf by the roll,
and deliver <u>anywhere</u> in the UK!

Price per roll: £4.75
(2 m × 2 m)

<u>Delivery Charges</u>:

Under 10 rolls: £9.25
10-20 rolls: £14.25
Over 20 rolls: £19.25

a)   What area of turf will Jordan need to order for his lawn?

....

....

....

....

....

....

....
                                                                                    (4 marks)

b)   How much will it cost Jordan to turf the lawn if he has the rolls delivered?

....

....

....

....

....

....

....
                                                                                    (4 marks)

6. Sunita is redesigning her garden and has drawn up a plan of it.

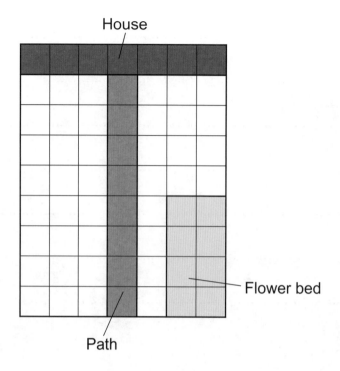

Key: Side of 1 square on the plan = 200 cm in the garden.

a) How wide is Sunita's garden in metres?

    ....

    ....

    (2 marks)

b) Sunita wants to put a 4 m × 4 m summer house in the garden.

    •   The summer house must be at least 4 m from the house.

    •   It can't be built on the path or the flower bed.

    Choose a place to put the summer house and draw the
    summer house to scale on the plan.

    (2 marks)

Task 3 — Health and Fitness

7.   Jane is making a display board for Local Leisure Ltd.

She has collected information from members on how much they exercise and their Body Mass Index (BMI). The information is shown in the table below.

Hours of exercise per week	10	9	8	7	12	8	6	9	9	8
BMI	20	21	23	25	16	24	28	22	23	25

a)   Using the information in the table, draw a graph or chart of BMI against number of hours of exercise on the grid below.

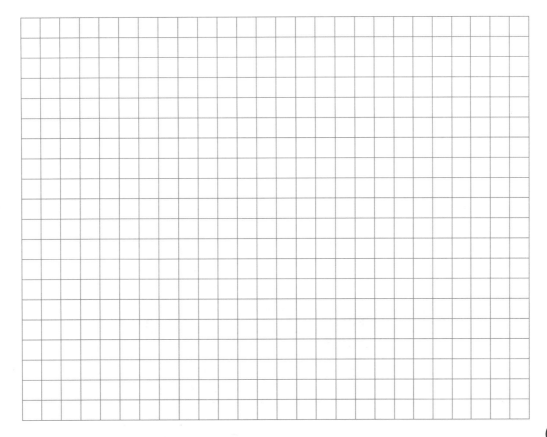

(3 marks)

b)   Using the information in your graph or chart, make one statement about the relationship between BMI and time spent exercising.

....

....

(1 mark)

8. Jane wants to work out her own BMI. She uses the following formula:

$$BMI = \frac{M}{(H^2)}$$

where M = body mass in kg
and H = height in m

a) Jane's body mass is 55 kg. She is 1.6 m tall. What is her BMI?

....

....

(2 marks)

b) Jane's friend has a BMI of 25.5. She is 1.55 m tall. What is her body mass?

Show a check of your calculation.

....

....

....

....

(4 marks)

The table below can be used as a guide to determine whether someone is underweight, normal weight, overweight or obese.

BMI	Weight Description
below 18.5	underweight
18.5 - 24.9	normal
25 - 29.9	overweight
30 - 40	moderately obese
above 40	severely obese

c) What weight description categories do Jane and her friend fall into?

....

....

(2 marks)

Task 4 — Going Out

9.   Mia and Deanne are planning a day in town.
     They want to see a fashion show at Bedhams and go to the 'Quick Flash Sale!'
     They also want to see 'Snow Age' at the cinema.
     The cinema is 1 mile away from Bedhams. They can walk at about 3 miles per hour.

Bedhams Department Store
Fashion Show: 10.00 – 11.00
12.30 – 13.30
Quick Flash Sale! starts at 15.30

Cinema Film Times
Snow Age: 11.10 – 13.10
11.30 – 13.30
14.00 – 16.00
14.30 – 16.30

a)   Draw up a timetable for the girls' day in the space below.

(3 marks)

b)   The girls want to have lunch at Bedhams before the Quick Flash Sale.
     How much time will they have? Explain your answer.

     ....

     ....

     ....

(1 mark)

10.   Hannah and Wayne are going to watch the film 'On the Ghost Trail' at the cinema on Minsterbury High Street. They want to catch the bus from Nauton Green.

Film Times:

On the Ghost Trail (160 mins*)
Starts: 6 pm

Shakespeare's Lovers (150 mins*)
Starts: 7.15 pm

In the Ghetto (125 mins*)
Starts: 9.45 pm

*Plus approx. 20 mins of trailers
at start of the screening.

Hastwick	1605	1705	1805
Nauton Green	1635	1735	1835
Minsterbury Castle St.	1650	1750	1850
Minsterbury High St.	1655	1755	1855
Minsterbury Bus Station	1705	1805	1905

Minsterbury Bus Station	1915	2015	2115*
Minsterbury High St.	1925	2025	2125
Minsterbury Castle St.	1930	2030	2130
Nauton Green	1945	2045	2145
Hastwick	2015	2105	2205

*Last Bus

a) It takes 10 minutes to walk to the bus stop in Nauton Green. What is the latest time
    Hannah and Wayne can set off to get to the cinema on time? Explain your answer.

    ....

    ....

    ....

    ....

    ....

    (2 marks)

b) Hannah is worried that they will miss the last bus home after the film.
    Will they be in time to catch it?

    ....

    ....

    ....

    ....

    ....

    ....

    (3 marks)

11.   Betty wants to visit the War Museum, Art Gallery and Science Museum.

Her friend will drop her off and pick her up from the War Museum,
and she will travel between each place by boat.

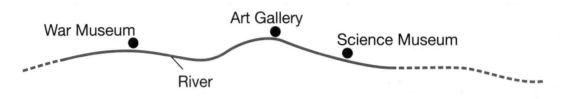

Map scale: 1 cm = 1.5 km

BOAT PRICES

Between:	Single:	Return:
War Museum and Art Gallery	£3.75	£7
Art Gallery and Science Museum	£2.20	£4
Science Museum and War Museum	£4.50	£8

ENTRY PRICES

War Museum — £4.50

Art Gallery — free

Science Museum — £5.90

a) If Betty buys her boat tickets in the cheapest way possible,
    what will be the total cost of her day trip?

    ....

    ....

    ....

    ....

    ....

    ....

    ....

    (3 marks)

b) How far is the boat journey between the Art Gallery and the Science Museum?
    Give your answer in miles. Distance in miles = distance in km × 0.6.

    ....

    ....

    ....

    ....

    ....

    ....

    (3 marks)

Task 5 — Decorating

12.   Teresa is painting her living room. She wants to know how much paint to buy.

1 litre of paint covers 12 m² with one coat.

Room measurements:
4 walls, each wall is 4 m by 3 m.
The room has 1 door, which is 1 m by 2 m,
and 2 windows, which are both 1 m by 2 m.

How many tins should Teresa buy to paint the room with three coats?

....

....

....

....

....

....

(3 marks)

13.   James is painting his kitchen light blue.

He needs to mix dark blue paint with white paint to make the right colour.

The paint should be mixed with a ratio of 1:2, blue:white.

The area to be painted is 36 m². 0.5 litres of paint will cover 1 square metre of wall.

The tins of paint hold 2 litres each.

How many tins of white paint will James need?

....

....

....

....

....

....

....

....

(3 marks)

14. Sandeep is tiling his bathroom. He works out that he will need to put up 80 tiles in total. He starts tiling at 1 pm.

    a) Sandeep puts up 30 tiles by 3 pm. If he continues to work at this pace, can he finish tiling the bathroom by 6 pm? Explain your answer.

....

....

....

....

....

(3 marks)

    b) Sandeep also needs to tile his shower room. He wants to create a symmetrical pattern, using three different tiles:

T1   T2   T3

The pattern will be 6 tiles wide and 4 tiles long. Sandeep wants to use equal numbers of each tile. He doesn't want any gaps between the tiles.

On the grid below, draw a symmetrical pattern that Sandeep could use.

(3 marks)

Task 6 — A Car Boot Sale

15.a) Dave is selling CDs, DVDs, books and comics at a car boot sale. He sells CDs for 50p, DVDs for £1, books for 30p and comics for 20p. Dave wants to make a table to keep track of how many of each item he has sold as he goes along. He also wants to be able to record the amount of money he has made at the end of the day.

Draw a table that Dave could use.

The table must have room to record:

- the items being sold (books, CDs, DVDs and comics)

- the price of each item

- the number of each item sold

- the amount of money he has made from each of CDs, books, DVDs and comics

- the total amount of money he has made

(4 marks)

b)   Chris is running a stall at the car boot sale. He packs some of the items he wants to sell into boxes, shown below. These boxes are then packed into crates.

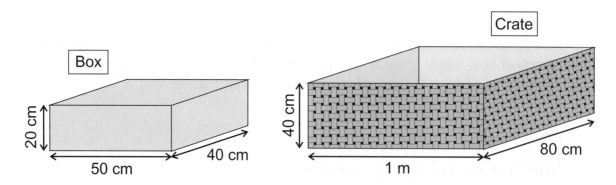

i)   How many boxes will Chris be able to fit into each crate?

....

....

....

....

(3 marks)

ii) Chris has run out of boxes and needs to make some more. Draw a net that Chris could use to make the box shown above. Write the dimensions on the net.

(2 marks)

c) Jess has made 15 bead necklaces to sell at the car boot sale.
The receipts for the materials she bought to make the necklaces are shown below:

necklace clasps	£11.25
thin leather cord	£3.80
Total	£15.05

Glass beads (large)	— £9.65
Glass beads (small)	— £6.10
Total	— £15.75

large red beads	£4.00
small blue beads	£1.60
small red beads	£1.60
painted beads	£2.50
Total	£9.70

Jess wants to make a 20% profit. What price will she need to sell each necklace for?

....

....

....

....

....

(3 marks)

Task 7 — City Planning

16.a) Craig is designing an office building. A sketch of one of Craig's ideas is shown below.

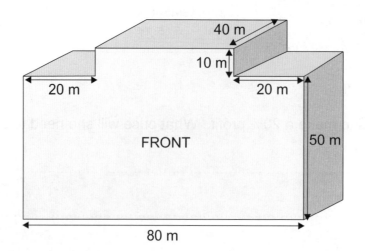

i) Craig needs accurate plans of the building to show to the town planners.

Draw a side view of the building above on the grid provided below.
You must clearly label the building's dimensions.

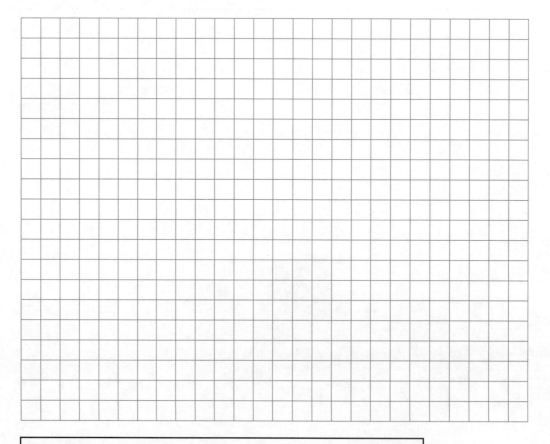

Key: Side of 1 square on the grid is 10 m on the building.

(2 marks)

ii) Craig has drawn plan views of two more of his ideas, shown below.
These show the buildings from above.

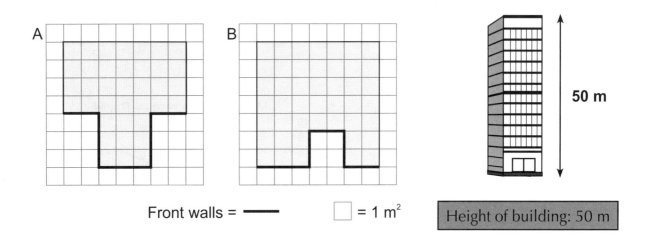

Front walls = ——   ☐ = 1 m²   Height of building: 50 m

Reinforced, toughened glass: £100 per m²

The front walls of the building will be made from glass.
How much extra would it cost to make the front walls of Building A
compared to Building B?

....

....

....

....

....

....

....

....

(5 marks)

b)   A local council is resurfacing a car park with concrete.

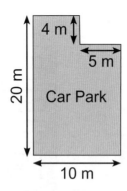

What will the total cost of the concrete be?

....

....

....

....

....

....

(3 marks)

c)   A housing committee are responsible for making sure there are enough 'low-cost' houses in a town.

Their annual report shows their targets and their results.

Price of houses built in 2012

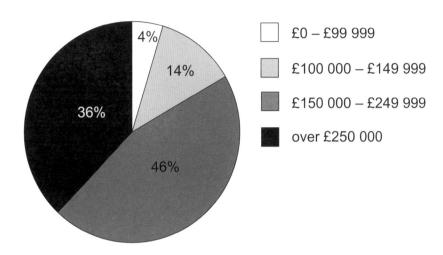

	£0 – £99 999
	£100 000 – £149 999
	£150 000 – £249 999
	over £250 000

Committee Targets

2012 target: 25% of new houses must be 'low-cost'.

'Low-cost' houses are houses that cost less than £150 000.

i) 3600 new houses were built in 2012.
    How many more low-cost houses should have been built to meet the target?

    ....

    ....

    ....

    ....

    ....

    ....

    ....

    (3 marks)

ii) 4200 new houses are going to be built next year.
    8 out of 10 of these will cost over £150 000 to buy.
    What percentage will be low-cost houses?

    ....

    ....

    ....

    ....

    ....

    (2 marks)

Task 8 — A Christmas Fair

17.   Colin has made a game for a Christmas fair. In a bag, he has 3 red balls, 5 green balls and 7 black balls. If you pick a red ball, you win a prize.

a) i)   If 140 people play Colin's game, how many people are likely to win?

....

....

....
(2 marks)

ii)   Colin wants to record the colour of ball picked each time the game is played. Draw a table that Colin could use to do this.

(2 marks)

b)   Adil has arranged a mini sports tournament for the fair.
He splits people into three teams and they play three games.
The scoring system is:

- 10 points for winning

- 5 points for second place

- 2 points for last place

i)   The table below shows the results for Game 1.

In Game 2, Team 2 won, Team 1 came second and Team 3 came last.
In Game 3, Team 1 won, with Team 2 coming second and Team 3 last.

Use these scores to complete the table.

	Game 1	Game 2	Game 3	Total
Team 1	5			
Team 2	2			
Team 3	10			

(3 marks)

ii) The team with the most points won the tournament.

Adil says that the team that won had both the highest mean score and the highest modal score. Is he correct? Explain your answer.

....

....

....

....

....

....

(3 marks)

c)   Yvonne is running a competition called 'Guess the Weight of the Sweets in the Jar'.
     The table below shows the first five guesses.

	Weight Guessed
Nick	3 lbs
Leila	1.6 kg
Carys	2.2 lbs
Evan	2500 g
Paul	32 oz

1 kg = 2.2 lbs

1 lb = 16 oz

The jar weighs 1.54 kg.

Of the people in the table, who came closest to guessing the correct weight?

....

....

....

....

....

....

....

....

....

(6 marks)

Answers — Practice Questions

Section One — Number

Page 2
Q1 14 034
Q2 154
 To check: 154 + 96 = 250
Q3 £59
Q4 Yes. He has 15 days' holiday left.

Page 4
Q1 250 g
Q2 £0.32 or 32p
 To check: 0.32 × 100 = 32
Q3 a) £24
 b) £84

Page 5
Q1 a) 289
 b) 1936
Q2 3
Q3 4

Page 7
Q1 2
Q2 22
Q3 17
Q4 105 miles

Page 9
Q1 Jess
Q2 a) Rachael
 b) -£331
Q3 12 °C

Page 10
Q1 -3 °C
Q2 1 °C

Page 11
Q1 a) $\dfrac{9}{13}$

 b) $\dfrac{4}{13}$

Page 12
Q1 12
Q2 10
Q3 a) 4
 b) 8

Page 13
Q1 £20
Q2 360 g
Q3 £1000

Page 15
Q1 18.75 or 18¾
Q2 4.75
Q3 It's quicker to change at Lancaster. This journey only takes 2.25 hours (2¼) compared to 2.5 (2½) hours.

Page 19
Q1 3.6
Q2 1.02
Q3 1.05 km, 1.2 km, 1.25 km, 1.75 km
Q4 No. She only has 43.8 points.
Q5 £238.32
Q6 18.75 hours or 18¾ hours
Q7 £0.80 or 80p
Q8 £7.89

Page 21
Q1 7.68
Q2 264
Q3 9
Q4 21
Q5 £14 700

Page 22
Q1 £72
Q2 £21 420
Q3 £36 750
Q4 455

Page 24
Q1 a) 0.75
 b) $\dfrac{1}{2}$

Q2 a) 80%
 b) 0.8
Q3 0.75 (¾ or 75% would also be correct).
Q4 20%

Page 25
Q1 $\dfrac{6}{15}$
Q2 A third off line rental. It saves you £4.20 a month compared to £3.25 a month for 25% off broadband.

Page 26
Q1 a) 15 out of 60 OR $\dfrac{15}{60}$

 (you could also put e.g. $\dfrac{5}{20}$ or $\dfrac{1}{4}$)

 b) 25 out of 60 OR $\dfrac{25}{60}$

 (you could also put $\dfrac{5}{12}$)

Q2 18 out of 27 OR $\dfrac{18}{27}$

 (you could also put e.g. $\dfrac{6}{9}$ or $\dfrac{2}{3}$)

Q3 4 out of 20 OR $\dfrac{4}{20}$

 (you could also put e.g. $\dfrac{2}{10}$ or $\dfrac{1}{5}$)

Page 29
Q1 300 ml
Q2 a) 48
 b) 72
Q3 300 g
Q4 2 litres
Q5 300

Page 31
Q1 750 g
Q2 187.5 ml
Q3 88.2 minutes or 88 minutes and 12 seconds or 1 hour 28 minutes and 12 seconds.
Q4 7 cards completed

Page 33
Q1 £40
Q2 £70
Q3 £67.50
Q4 £33 (£20 before midnight, plus £13 after midnight)
Q5 £68

Page 36
Q1 a) 7
 b) 14
Q2 4
Q3 £320

Page 38
Q1 6 kilometres
Q2 60 cm

Section Two — Measure

Page 42
Q1 7500 m
Q2 6.4 kg
Q3 0.56 L
Q4 33 lbs
Q5 6.2 miles
Q6 £300
Q7 a) 0.2 L
   b) 200 ml
Q8 190.5 cm

Page 45
Q1 a) 26 cm
   b) 108 mm
Q2 a) 3.6 cm
   b) 1.8 cm
   c) the circumference
Q3 a) 4.9 m
   b) 8.5 m
   c) 31.4 m
   If you got the wrong answer for part a) and b), you'll have got a different answer to part c).
Q4 37 cm

Page 48
Q1 9 strips.
Q2 105 squares of turf.
Q3 70 desks
   If you start with desks right against a side wall, you can fit 7 desks in a row across the hall. If you start with desks right up against the front wall of the hall, you can fit ten rows going the length of the hall. 7 × 10 = 70 desks. If you left a gap at the front or side of the hall you'll have a slightly different answer.

Page 50
Q1 a) 4 cm²
   b) 11.77 m²
Q2 525 cm²
Q3 0.81 m²
Q4 a) 36.76 cm²
   b) 108 cm²

Page 52
Q1 10.8 cm²
Q2 3848.45... mm² (or 3846.5 mm² if you used 3.14 for π)

Page 55
Q1 85 cm²
Q2 £214.50
   To answer this question you need to start by working out the total area of floor = (7 x 3) + (6 x 2) = 33 m². Then work out the amount of concrete you need by multiplying this area by the amount of concrete per m². This is 33 m² x 0.1 = 3.3 m³. The cost of this concrete is 3.3 m³ x £65 = £214.50.

Page 57
Q1 a) 9000 cm³
   b) 70 000 mm³
Q2 0.168 m³ or 168 000 cm³
Q3 1 bag

Page 60
Q1 a) 1642p
   b) £2.10
Q2 The 12 pack is the best value for money. (£0.52 per can. The price per can of the 6 pack is £0.53.)
Q3 Michelle as the 14 g jar is the best value. (It costs 6.79p per gram. The 7 g jar costs 8.57p per gram.)

Page 62
Q1 The free fitting offer will save Gillian the most money. (£120 off. The 20% off offer only saves £103.30.)
Q2 £0.45 or 45p
Q3 a) £1.30
   b) 50%
Q4 Luke should charge £2.43 for each cake to make 35% profit.

Page 65
Q1 a) 8:30 am
   b) 7:57 pm
Q2 a) 18:15
   b) 00:03
Q3 No (22:59 is 10:59 pm).
Q4 2 hours and 30 minutes (2½ hours) or 150 minutes.
Q5 1 hour and 49 minutes (109 minutes)
Q6 32 minutes
Q7 8:02 pm

Page 66
Q8 18:55 (6:55 pm)
Q9 Yes, Phillip could be at the meeting place at 7:45 pm (19.45).
Q10 She should leave home by 11:50 am.

Page 69
Q1 a) The 15:08 train.
   b) 15:49
Q2 14:00 on Tuesday or 09:00 on Thursday or 11:00 on Friday.
Q3 E.g.

	Night 1	Night 2
First half	Streetdance	Camberwell
	Salsa Stream	Super Eights
	Super Eights	Havanas
	Interval	
Second half	DUBDS	Xtreme Beats
	Havanas	DUBDS
	Mirror Ball	Salsa Stream

Other answers and layouts are possible. Streetdance must appear on night 1 only and Xtreme Beats on night 2 only. Camberwell must not appear in the same half as Streetdance or Xtreme Beats.

Section Three — Shape and Space

Page 72
Q1 E.g. 10 cm by 30 cm by 15 cm
Q2 For example:

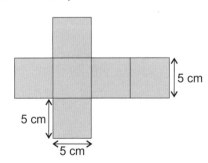

Q3 For example:

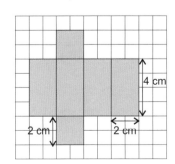

Page 73

Q1

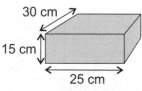

Page 74

Q1 For example:

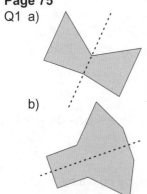

The easiest way to send the books is to stack them on top of each other. So the box needs to be as long and as wide as the biggest book and as high as all 3.

Page 75

Q1 a)

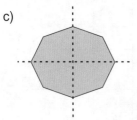

b)

c)

Q2 a)

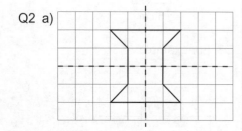

b)

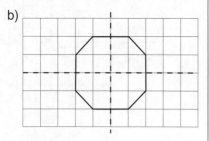

Page 76

Q1 For example:

C	B	B	C
D	A	A	D
D	A	A	D
C	B	B	C

Other symmetrical patterns are possible.

Page 79

Q1 For example:

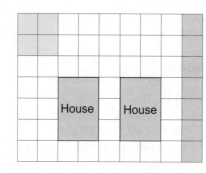

Other positions possible.

Q2 a)

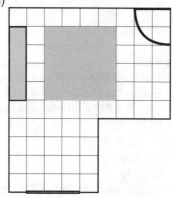

The table can go anywhere in the shaded area.

b) No (it would block the door/window).

Page 81

Q1 a) 4 cm
b) 20 km
Q2 a) 8 miles
b) 26 miles

Section Four — Handling Data

Page 83

Q1 a) 1.2 miles
b) Hotel C
c) Hotel A

Q2 a) 42.5 miles
b) 27.6 miles
c) 80.1 miles

Page 85

Q1

Employee	Standard days off	Extra days off	Total days off
Mike	25	5	30
Sharon	25	2	27
Lucy	25	0	25
Phoebe	25	1	26

Q2

	Number of guests	Number of platters required	Total cost of platters (£)
Wedding 1	120	18	360
Wedding 2	80	12	240

Q3

	Interior score	Exterior score	Mech-anical score	Number of modifi-cations	Total score
Car 1	8	7	7	0	22
Car 2	7	9	9	2	23
Car 3	6	9	7	1	21

Page 86

Q1 a)

Type of cake	Tally	Frequency
Birthday	|||||	5
Wedding	||	2
Christening	||	2
Retirement			1
Christmas	|||	3
		Total 13

b) 5
c) 13

Answers — Practice Questions

Page 88

Q1 For example

Item	Quantity	Price	Total cost of items
		Total cost of order	

There are other ways of drawing this table. Just make sure you've left space for all of the details you were asked for.

Q2 For example

Guest name	Starter			Main Course			Dessert		
	1	2	3	1	2	3	1	2	3
Total									

There are other ways of drawing this table. As long as you have space for all of the details listed then the table will be correct.

Page 89

Q1 a) 3
   b) Yellow
   c) 17

Page 91

Q1 a) 6000
   b) 3000
   c) 4000
   d) Year 5
Q2 a) 70%
   b) 20%
   c) Year 3
   d) The percentage of flights to places in the UK stayed the same from year 1 to year 2 and then decreased from 30% of flights to 20% of flights from year 2 to year 3.

Page 94

Q1 a) 8 km
   b) 7.5 miles
   c) 9 miles
Q2 a) 130 litres
   b) 10 litres
   c) Day 1 (40 litres)
Q3 a) 10 minutes
   b) 13 minutes
   c) About 1.5 (1½) minutes

Page 96

Q1 a) Shop 2
   b) 50%
   c) 25%
Q2 a) i) 50 strikes
      ii) 25 strikes
      iii) 45 strikes
   b) 120 strikes
   If you got the wrong answers for any of the parts of a), you'll have got a different answer to part b).

Page 100

Q1 a) 120

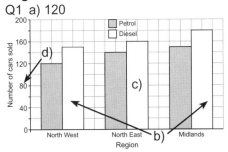

Q2 A graph to show the amount of hot water remaining from 06:00 to 18:00

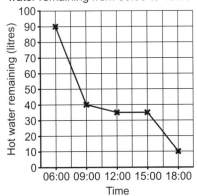

Page 103

Q1 Call Centre A because they answered a higher percentage of calls in under 45 seconds (the target time) in 2 of the 3 months. Call centre B only managed the same percentage of calls answered in the target time as call centre A in 1 month (Feb).

Q2 The graph shows that as speed increases, the exterior noise level also increases.

Q3 For example — In general, the more hours someone works in a week, the higher their annual income is. Martha doesn't fit into this pattern though — she earns less than Joseph and Eugenia even though she works more hours.

Page 106

Q1 £3797.10
Q2 1880 kg
Q3 38 minutes
Q4 a) 8 boxes
   b) 7 boxes

Page 107

Q1 a) 13
   b) 45
Q2 a) 3.3 miles
   b) No (it is less than the largest distance of 5.5 miles)

Page 109

Q1 a) Range = £118
      Mean = £554
   b) Range = £95
      Mean = £680
   c) On average Fly Well holidays are cheaper than City Escapes holidays — the mean price of a Fly Well holiday (£607.50) is less than the mean price of a City Escapes holiday (£645).

Page 112

Q1 No, he is not. It's not impossible for the weather to be warm and sunny in December, it's just very unlikely.

Q2 $\frac{6}{24}$ or $\frac{3}{12}$ or $\frac{2}{8}$ or $\frac{1}{4}$ or 0.25 or 25%

Q3 $\frac{30}{90}$ or $\frac{3}{9}$ or $\frac{1}{3}$

Q4 a) $\frac{4}{16}$ or $\frac{2}{8}$ or $\frac{1}{4}$, 0.25 and 25%

   b) $\frac{12}{16}$ or $\frac{6}{8}$ or $\frac{3}{4}$, 0.75 and 75%

Q5 a) $\frac{8}{10}$ or $\frac{4}{5}$, 0.8 and 80%

   b) Probability of picking out a quartz necklace

   0 ———————————— 0.8 1.0

Answers — Test-style Questions

Task 1 — Banking and Finance (Page 114)

1   a) 3 × £23 500 = £70 500 *(1 mark)*. One fifth of
       £55 000 = 1 ÷ 5 × £55 000 = £11 000 *(1 mark)*.
       So Sean can borrow enough money for the flat, but
       his deposit isn't large enough, so he can't buy it
       (1 mark).
   b) 2½ × £23 500 = £58 750 *(1 mark)*.
       15% of £55 000 = 15 ÷ 100 × £55 000 = £8250
       (1 mark). Sean can borrow enough money for the
       flat and his deposit is large enough, so he can buy
       the flat *(1 mark)*.

2   a) £16 000 − £7475 = £8525
       So Danni will have to pay 20% of £8525 *(1 mark)*.
       20 ÷ 100 × 8525 = £1705 income tax each year
       (1 mark).
   b) £16 000 − £8105 = £7895
       So Danni will now have to pay 20% of £7895
       (1 mark).
       20 ÷ 100 × 7895 = £1579 *(1 mark)*
       This is £1705 − £1579 = £126 less tax than before
       (1 mark).

   *If you got the wrong answer for part a), you'll have got
   a different answer to part b). As long as your working is
   correct, you should still get the marks.*

3   Annual interest rate on a loan of £6750 is 15%.
    15% of £6750 = 15 ÷ 100 × 6750 = £1012.50 *(1 mark)*
    Total to pay back = £6750 + £1012.50 = £7762.50
    (1 mark)
    So each month, Emily will have to pay:
    £7762.50 ÷ 12 months = £646.875 = £646.88 to the
    nearest penny *(1 mark)*.

Task 2 — Landscape Gardening (Page 119)

4   a) Diameter of the pond = 2 m. So the perimeter of
       the pond = π × 2 OR 3.14 × 2 *(1 mark)* = 6.28 m
       (1 mark). 6.28 m × 100 = 628 cm *(1 mark)*.
       Number of tiles needed =
       628 cm ÷ 10 cm = 62.8 tiles (or 63 tiles to the
       nearest whole tile) *(1 mark)*
       There are 10 tiles per box, so the number of boxes
       needed = 63 ÷ 10 = 6.3. So Harry needs to buy 7
       boxes of tiles *(1 mark)*.
   b) VAT is 20%. 20% of £4 is 20 ÷ 100 × 4 = £0.80 so
       each box will cost £4 + £0.80 = £4.80 *(1 mark)*.
       7 boxes of tiles are needed, 7 × £4.80 = £33.60
       (1 mark).

   *If you got the wrong answer for part a), you'll have got
   a different answer to part b). As long as your working is
   correct, you should still get the marks.*

5   a) Split the lawn into rectangles and work out the area
       of the different rectangles. For example:
       9 × 5 = 45 m² *(1 mark)*
       12 − 5 = 7 m *(1 mark)*
       7 × 5 = 35 m² *(1 mark)*
       So the area of turf needed = 45 + 35 = 80 m²
       (1 mark)

*There are other ways you could have worked this out.
For example, found the total area of the garden and
then taken away the area of the flower bed.*

   b) Each roll will cover 2 m × 2 m = 4 m² *(1 mark)*
       80 m² ÷ 4 m² = 20 rolls *(1 mark)*
       Cost of 20 rolls = £4.75 × 20 = £95 *(1 mark)*
       Cost of delivery for 20 rolls = £14.25
       Total cost = £95 + £14.25 = £109.25 *(1 mark)*

6   a) Sunita's garden is 7 squares wide.
       The side of 1 square = 200 cm, so Sunita's
       garden is: 7 × 200 = 1400 cm wide *(1 mark)*
       To convert cm to m, divide by 100.
       So Sunita's garden is 1400 ÷ 100 = 14 m wide
       (1 mark)
   b) The summer house can be built anywhere in the
       grey area to the left of the path OR anywhere
       in the smaller grey area to the right of the path,
       above the flower bed (see below). It should be
       2 squares wide and 2 squares long. *(1 mark
       for correct positioning of the summer house,
       1 mark for a summer house of the correct size)*

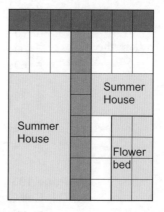

Task 3 — Health and Fitness (Page 123)

7   a) For example:

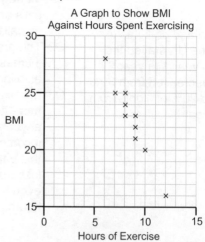

   *(1 mark for choosing a sensible scale for the
   axes, 1 mark for labelling the axes and giving
   the graph a title, 1 mark for correctly plotting
   all data points)*

b) The more time spent exercising, the lower a person's BMI *(1 mark)*.

8 a) BMI = M ÷ H²
So Jane's BMI = 55 ÷ (1.6²) = 21.48
(1 mark for correct calculation, 1 mark for correct answer)

b) BMI = M ÷ H²
So BMI × H² = M
Jane's friend's height = 1.55 m
Her BMI = 25.5
So her mass = 25.5 × (1.55²) = 61.26 kg
(1 mark for BMI × H² = M, 1 mark for 25.5 × (1.55²), 1 mark for 61.26 kg or 61.3 kg)
To check your answer, do the reverse of the calculation: BMI = M ÷ H² = 61.26 ÷ (1.55²) = 25.498 = 25.5 *(1 mark)*

c) Jane is normal weight *(1 mark)*. Her friend is overweight *(1 mark)*.

If you got the wrong answer for part a), you'll have got a different answer to part c) for Jane. As long as your working is correct, you should still get the marks.

Task 4 — Going Out (Page 125)

9 a) To be at the Quick Flash Sale at 15.30, they need to see either the 11.10 or 11.30 showing of Snow Age. Both of these overlap with the 12.30 fashion show, so they have to go to the 10.00 fashion show. This finishes at 11.00. It's 1 mile from Bedhams to the cinema and they can walk at 3 miles per hour. 1 hour is 60 minutes. To work out how long it'll take them to walk 1 mile: 60 mins ÷ 3 = 20 minutes. So they will only be able to make the 11.30 film showing.
Timetable:
10.00 — Fashion Show
11.30 — Snow Age
15.30 — Quick Flash Sale
(1 mark for each activity included in the timetable at the correct time.)

You might have drawn your timetable a bit differently to this one. That's fine, as long as the times are right, you'll get the marks.

b) The film finishes at 13.30 and it takes 20 minutes to walk to Bedhams, so they will arrive at 13.50. The sale starts at 15.30 so they will have 1 hour, 40 minutes for lunch *(1 mark)*.

10 a) Hannah and Wayne should get the 1735 bus from Nauton Green as it will get them to the cinema at 1755 in time for the 6 pm (1800) film *(1 mark)*. They need to set off 10 minutes before this, which is 1725 *(1 mark)*.

b) The film plus trailers will last:
20 minutes + 160 minutes = 180 minutes / 3 hours *(1 mark)*. Starting at 6 pm, it should finish at 9 pm (which is 2100) *(1 mark)*. The last bus leaves Minsterbury High Street at 2125, so yes, they should be in time to catch it *(1 mark)*.

11 a) Betty can either buy three single boat tickets, or two return tickets.
Single Tickets:
War Museum – Art Gallery: £3.75.
Art Gallery – Science Museum: £2.20.
Science Museum – War Museum: £4.50.
So total = £3.75 + £2.20 + £4.50 = £10.45.
Return Tickets:
Option 1: Return tickets between the War Museum and Art Gallery, and between the Art Gallery and Science Museum which costs £7 + £4 = £11.
Option 2: Return tickets between the War Museum and Science Museum and between the War Museum and Art Gallery, which costs £8 + £4 = £12.
So it is cheaper to buy single tickets.
Total cost of boats and museum entry = £10.45 + £4.50 + £5.90 = £20.85.
(1 mark for comparing at least two ticket combinations, 1 mark for the decision that it is cheaper to buy 3 single tickets, 1 mark for £20.85)

b) Distance between Art Gallery and Science Museum on the map = 2 cm.
Map scale: 1 cm = 1.5 km
So distance in real life = 2 × 1.5 = 3 km *(1 mark)*
Distance (in miles) = number of km × 0.6
= 3 km × 0.6 *(1 mark)* = 1.8 miles *(1 mark)*

Task 5 — Decorating (Page 130)

12 Each wall is 4 m × 3 m = 12 m². 12 m² × 4 = 48 m². The door is 2 m × 1 m = 2 m². Two windows, both 2 m × 1 m = 2m², so 2 × 2 m² = 4 m².
Total wall area = 48 m² − 2 m² − 4 m² = 42 m²
(1 mark)
1 litre covers 12 m², so Teresa will need:
42 m² ÷ 12 m² = 3.5 litres for 1 coat.
For 3 coats of paint, Teresa will need:
3 × 3.5 litres = 10.5 litres *(1 mark)*.
Each tin is 2 litres, so she will need:
10.5 ÷ 2 = 5.25 tins of paint, so 6 tins in total *(1 mark)*.

13 Area of room = 36 m²
James needs 0.5 litres of paint per square metre, so he needs to make:
36 × 0.5 = 18 litres of light blue paint *(1 mark)*.
The total number of parts in the ratio = 1 + 2 = 3. So each part is: 18 ÷ 3 = 6 litres of paint *(1 mark)*.
James needs 2 parts white paint, which is:
6 × 2 = 12 litres.
Each tin holds 2 litres, so he needs:
12 ÷ 2 = 6 tins *(1 mark)*.

14 a) Sandeep has put up 30 tiles in 2 hours (1 pm til 3 pm = 2 hours), so he is working at a pace of:
30 ÷ 2 = 15 tiles per hour *(1 mark)*.
In another 3 hours (3 pm til 6 pm = 3 hours), he can put up: 3 × 15 = 45 tiles *(1 mark)*.
In total, by 6 pm he will have put up 30 + 45 = 75 tiles. So, no, he won't finish tiling the bathroom by 6 pm *(1 mark)*.

b) For example:

T1	T3	T2	T2	T3	T1
T2	T3	T1	T1	T3	T2
T2	T3	T1	T1	T3	T2
T1	T3	T2	T2	T3	T1

(1 mark for a pattern measuring 6 tiles by 4 tiles, 1 mark for using 8 of each type of tile, 1 mark for a symmetrical pattern with no gaps)

Task 6 — A Car Boot Sale (Page 133)

15 a) For example,

Item	Price	Tally	Total sold	Money made
CD	£0.50			
DVD	£1.00			
Books	£0.30			
Comics	£0.20			
				Total:

(1 mark for a clearly structured and labelled table, 1 mark for space for recording items and prices, 1 mark for space for recording numbers sold and money made, 1 mark for space for recording total money made.)

b) i) Calculate the volume of a box:
Volume = length × width × height
= 40 × 50 × 20 = 40 000 cm² *(1 mark)*
Calculate the volume of a crate:
To convert m into cm, times by 100:
1 × 100 = 100 cm.
Volume = 100 × 80 × 40 = 320 000 cm² *(1 mark)*
He will be able to fit:
320 000 ÷ 40 000 = 8 boxes into each crate *(1 mark)*.

There's more than one way to work this out, so don't worry if you did it differently. As long as your method was correct, you'll still get the marks.

ii) For example:

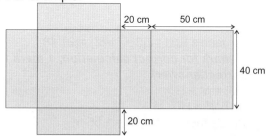

(1 mark for a correctly drawn net — with or without the lid, 1 mark for at least three correct dimensions labelled on the net)

c) Total cost of buying the materials =
£15.05 + £15.75 + £9.70 = £40.50 *(1 mark)*.
Jess wants to make a 20% profit.
20% of £40.50 = 20 ÷ 100 × £40.50 = £8.10
So Jess would need to sell all the necklaces for:
£40.50 + £8.10 = £48.60 *(1 mark)*.
So she needs to sell each necklace for:
£48.60 ÷ 15 = £3.24 *(1 mark)*.

You might have worked out the actual cost per necklace first (£2.70) and then added on 20% to get the price she needed to sell it at. As long as your method was correct, you'll still get the marks.

Task 7 — City Planning (Page 136)

16 a) i)

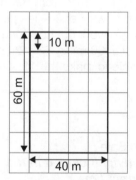

(1 mark for a correctly drawn view, 1 mark for correctly labelled dimensions.)

ii) Length of front walls of building A =
2 m + 3 m + 3 m + 3 m + 2 m = 13 m *(1 mark)*.
Length of front walls of building B =
3 m + 2 m + 2 m + 2 m + 2 m = 11 m *(1 mark)*.
Both buildings are 50 m high.
Building A would need:
50 × 13 m = 650 m² of glass
Which would cost:
650 × £100 = £65 000 *(1 mark)*.
Building B would need:
50 × 11 m = 550 m² of glass
Which would cost:
550 × £100 = £55 000 *(1 mark)*.
Building A would cost
£65 000 − £55 000 = £10 000 more *(1 mark)*.

There are other ways of calculating how much more the front walls of building A would cost, you don't need to have used the same working as above to get full marks.

b) Split the car park into two rectangles.
For example, area of bottom rectangle
= 10 m × 16 m = 160 m²
Area of top rectangle = 4 m × 5 m = 20 m² *(1 mark)*.
So total area of car park
= 160 m² + 20 m² = 180 m² *(1 mark)*.
Reading off the graph, 180 m² of concrete would
cost £7000 *(1 mark)*.

*There's more than one way to work out the area of the
car park, so don't worry if you did it differently. As long
as your method was correct, you'll still get the marks.*

c) i) The houses that would be classed as
low-cost are the ones in the categories
£0 - £99 999 and £100 000 - £149 999. This
is 4% + 14% = 18% of the houses built in 2012
(1 mark).
18% of 3600 is: 18 ÷ 100 × 3600 = 648.
25% of 3600 is: 25 ÷ 100 × 3600 = 900 *(1 mark)*.
900 − 648 = 252 extra houses needed to have
been built to reach the target *(1 mark)*.

*You could also answer this question by working out that
7% more houses needed to have been built, and that 7%
of 3600 is 252.*

ii) 8 out of 10 will cost over £150 000, so 2
out of 10 will be low-cost *(1 mark)*. So
2 ÷ 10 × 100 = 20% will be low-cost *(1 mark)*.

Task 8 — A Christmas Fair (Page 141)

17 a) i) Probability of drawing a red ball / winning = $\frac{3}{15}$ or
$\frac{1}{5}$ *(1 mark)*.

So number of people likely to win out of
140 people = 3 ÷ 15 × 140 = 28 *(1 mark)*.

ii) For example:

Colour Ball	Tally
Red	
Green	
Black	

*(1 mark for choosing any sensible way of
recording the number of each colour ball
picked, 1 mark for correctly labelled columns
and rows)*

b) i)

	Game 1	Game 2	Game 3	Total
Team 1	5	5	10	20
Team 2	2	10	5	17
Team 3	10	2	2	14

*(1 mark for each correctly filled in column.
Maximum marks = 3.)*

ii) Team 1 had a mean score of:
20 ÷ 3 = 6.67.
Team 2 had a mean score of:
17 ÷ 3 = 5.67.
Team 3 had a mean score of:
14 ÷ 3 = 4.67.
So Team 1 had the highest mean score
(1 mark).
The modal score for Team 1 was 5.
There was no modal score for Team 2.
The modal score for Team 3 was 2.
So Team 1 had the highest modal score
(1 mark). So yes, Adil is right *(1 mark)*.

c) The jar weighs 1.54 kg, so convert all the weights
guessed to kg.
Nick (3 lbs).
To find how many kg are in 3 lbs, divide 1 kg by
2.2, then multiply by 3:
1 ÷ 2.2 × 3 = 1.36 kg *(1 mark)*.
Carys (2.2 lbs).
1 kg = 2.2 lbs, so Carys' guess = 1 kg *(1 mark)*.
Evan (2500 g).
Convert from g to kg:
2500 ÷ 1000 = 2.5 kg *(1 mark)*.
Paul (32 oz).
16 oz = 1 lbs. So 32 oz = 2 lbs *(1 mark)*.
To find how many kg are in 2 lbs, divide 1 kg by
2.2, then multiply by 2:
1 ÷ 2.2 × 2 = 0.9 kg *(1 mark)*.
Leila came closest to guessing the correct weight
(1 mark).

Glossary

12-hour clock

The 12 hour clock goes from 12:00 am (midnight) to 11:59 am (one minute before noon), and then from 12:00 pm (noon) till 11:59 pm (one minute before midnight).

24-hour clock

The 24 hour clock goes from 00:00 (midnight) to 23:59 (one minute before the next midnight).

2D object

An object with 2 dimensions, i.e. a flat object.

3D object

An object with 3 dimensions, i.e. a solid object.

Area

How much surface a shape covers.

Average

A number that summarises a lot of data.

Axis

A line along the bottom and up the left-hand side of most graphs and charts.

Bar Chart

A chart which shows information using bars of different heights.

Capacity

How much something will hold. For example, a beaker with a capacity of 200 ml can hold 200 ml of liquid.

Certain

When something will definitely happen.

Circumference

The perimeter (distance around the outside) of a circle.

Decimal Number

A number with a decimal point (.) in it. For example, 0.75.

Diameter

The distance from one side of a circle to the other, going straight through the middle. The diameter is twice the radius.

Dimension

A number that tells you about the size of an object. For example, its length.

Even Chance

When something is as likely to happen as it is not to happen.

Formula

A rule for working out an amount.

Fraction

A way of showing parts of a whole. For example: ¼ (one quarter).

Frequency Table

A tally chart with an extra column that shows the total of each tally (the frequencies).

Impossible

When there's no chance at all of something happening.

Length

How long something is. Length can be measured in different units, for example, millimetres (mm), centimetres (cm), or metres (m).

Likely

When something isn't certain, but there's a high chance it will happen.

Line Graph

A graph which shows data using a line.

Line of Symmetry

A shape with a line of symmetry has two halves that are mirror images of each other. If the shape is folded along this line, the two sides will fold exactly together.

Map Scale

A number line that tells you how far a given distance on a map is in real life.

Mean

A type of average. To calculate the mean you add up all the numbers and divide the total by how many numbers there are.

Median

A type of average. The median is the middle value of a set of data when the values are arranged in size order.

Mileage Chart

A type of table that shows you the distance between different places.

Mixed Fraction

When you have a whole number and a fraction together. For example: 2¼ (two and a quarter).

Mode

A type of average. The mode is the most common value that appears in a set of data.

Negative number

A number less than zero. For example, -2.

Net

A 3D shape folded out flat. You can use a net to help you make a 3D object. For example, you can use a net to make a box.

Percentage

A way of showing how many parts you have out of 100. So twenty percent (20%) is the same as 20 parts out of 100.

Perimeter

The distance around the outside of a shape.

Pictogram

A chart that uses pictures or symbols to show how many of something there are.

Pie Chart

A circular chart that is divided into sections (that look like slices of a pie). The size of each section depends on how much or how many of something it represents.

Plan

A diagram to show the layout of an area. For example, the layout of objects in a room.

Probability

The likelihood (or chance) of an event happening or not.

Profit

The difference between the cost of making something and the price it's sold for.

Proportion

A way of showing how much of one part there is compared to the whole thing. For example, if there are 4 towels and 1 of them is white then the proportion of white towels is 1 in 4.

Radius

The distance from the side of a circle to the middle. The radius is half the diameter.

Range

The difference between the biggest and smallest numbers in a data set.

Ratio

A way of showing how many things of one type there are compared to another.
For example, if there are 3 red towels to every 1 white towel then the ratio of red to white towels is 3 : 1.

Square Number

A number multiplied by itself. For example: 5 squared (5^2) is the same as 5×5.

Surface Area

The total area of the sides of a shape.

Symmetry

See line of symmetry.

Table

A way of showing data. In a table, data is arranged into columns and rows.

Tally Chart

A chart used for putting data into different categories. You use tally marks (lines) to record each piece of data in the chart.

Unit

A way of showing what type of number you've got. For example, metres (m) or grams (g).

Unlikely

When something isn't impossible, but it probably won't happen.

Volume

The amount of space something takes up.

Weight

How heavy something is. Grams (g) and kilograms (kg) are common units for weight.

Index

Symbols

12-hour clock 63

24-hour clock 63

2D objects 70

3D objects 70, 71, 73, 74

π (pi) 51, 52

A

adding 1, 2, 18

areas 49-55

    of circles 51, 52

    of squares and
    rectangles 49

    of triangles 51

averages 104-106, 108, 109

    mean 104, 105, 109

    median 105

    mode 106

axes 89

B

bar charts 89, 90, 97, 99

    composite bar charts 90

    drawing bar charts 97

    dual bar charts 90, 99

brackets 6, 7

C

calculators 6, 7

capacity 40

charts 82, 83, 86, 89, 90,
    95, 97, 99

    bar charts 89, 90, 97, 99

    mileage charts 82, 83

    pie charts 95

    tally charts 86

checking your answer 2, 3

circles 44, 51, 52

circumference 44

composite bar charts 90

D

decimals 16-18, 23-25

diameter 44

dimensions 70, 74

discounts 13

dividing 3, 5, 18

dual bar charts 90, 99

F

formulas 32-38

    formulas in words 32

    rearranging formulas 36-38

fractions 11-15, 23-25

    mixed fractions 14, 15

frequency tables 86

G

graphs 92, 93, 98, 99, 101

I

interpreting data 101, 102

L

lengths 39, 43, 44, 46, 47

line graphs 92, 93, 98, 99,
    101

    drawing line graphs 98

lines of symmetry 75, 76

M

maps 80

mean 104, 105, 109

median 105

mileage charts 82, 83

mixed fractions 14, 15

mode 106

money 58-61

multiplying 3, 4, 18

N

negative numbers 8

nets 70, 71

number lines 8

P

percentages 20-23, 25

    percentage decrease 22

    percentage increase 21

perimeters 43, 44

pi (π) 51, 52

pictograms 95

pie charts 95

plans 77, 78

price per gram 59

price per item 59

probability 110, 111

profit 61

proportions 26, 30, 31

R

radius 44

range 107, 108

ratios 27, 28

rounding 16, 17

S

scales 9, 10, 80

    map scales 80

    reading scales 9, 10

scaling up and down 30

squaring numbers 4

subtracting 1, 2, 18

surface area 55

symmetry 75, 76

T

tables 82-87 102

    drawing tables 86, 87

tally charts 86

thermometers 9, 10

time 63, 64, 67, 68

timetables 67, 68

triangles 51

U

units 39-41, 49, 56, 58

    converting between units 41

    of area 49

    of capacity 40

    of length 39

    of money 58

    of volume 56

V

value for money 59

volumes 56

W

weight 40